THE VEIL OF MONEY

THE
VEIL OF MONEY

BY

A. C. PIGOU, M.A.

EMERITUS PROFESSOR OF POLITICAL ECONOMY
IN THE UNIVERSITY OF CAMBRIDGE
AUTHOR OF "THE ECONOMICS OF WELFARE", ETC.

GREENWOOD PRESS, PUBLISHERS
WESTPORT, CONNECTICUT

Library of Congress Cataloging in Publication Data

Pigou, Arthur Cecil, 1879-1959.
    The veil of money.

    Reprint of the 1949 ed. published by Macmillan,
London.
    1. Money. 2. Income. I. Title.
HG221.P6 1979   332.4   78-10214
ISBN 0-313-20742-9

Reprinted by permission of the Macmillan Press.

Reprinted in 1979 by Greenwood Press, Inc.
51 Riverside Avenue, Westport, CT 06880

Printed in the United States of America

10 9 8 7 6 5 4 3 2 1

PREFACE

In starting this book I had intended to write something thoroughly elementary, on a level with my *Income, an Introduction to Economics*. As things have turned out, portions, particularly some of the chapters (*e.g.* Chapter VI) of Part II, are substantially harder than anything to be found there. The book is still an 'introduction' in the sense that my larger works are not, but it is an introduction only suitable for students and other persons prepared to make some intellectual effort. Moreover, the book is general and academic in character. It is not a discussion of current problems. Some readers confronted with it can hardly fail to " regret that the writer has thrown little light, or at all events little direct light, on the grave economic difficulties with which our country is at present confronted " — or some other such cliché. Alas, I must leave them to their regret. An author is entitled to choose in his own topics, and potential readers who prefer other topics have a very simple remedy. I have to thank Professor D. H. Robertson, who very kindly read an early draft of the book in typescript and helped me with a number of valuable comments.

A. C. P.

King's College, Cambridge
October 1947

v

CONTENTS

PART I
MONEY

CHAPTER I

THE DEFINITION OF MONEY

IN the heyday of the gold standard an ordinary Englishman, if asked to define a pound sterling, would have pointed to a sovereign, said that that was a pound sterling, and stopped there. Now he would be more hesitant. There are no sovereigns to be pointed at. We might, perhaps, be inclined to say: "Very well then, a pound note is a pound sterling". But, looking at the note, we read, "Bank of England promise to pay the Bearer on demand the sum of one pound". The note cannot then itself be a pound sterling. Is the old sovereign? If this were so, then, in order to discharge a debt of £100 contracted at no matter what date, the debtor would need to hand over the gold content, or the value of the gold content, of 100 pre-war sovereigns; he could not clear himself by handing over 100 one-pound notes, which, of course, are now worth very much less than that. But in fact he *can* clear himself under English law by handing over 100 one-pound notes. It follows that a pound sterling is not a pre-war sovereign, and we have seen that it cannot be a one-pound note. What then precisely is it?

A pound sterling is not a thing at all. It is a name handed down in history. It is open to the government to proclaim at any time that a coin constituted in such-and-such a way, or a paper note on which such-and-such a device is printed — or, if it should so choose, a peach or a strawberry — is *equivalent to* a pound sterling; so that

3

debts falling due, that were contracted in terms of sterling, are legally acquitted by a transfer from debtor to creditor of the appropriate number of these things. If presently the government chooses to proclaim something else equivalent to a pound sterling, debts contracted in sterling, that fall due after this second proclamation, are then legally discharged by transfers of the appropriate number of units of this something else.

This is an extremely important principle. It entails that, when a government devalues its country's currency, it at the same time devalues in an equal proportion its own and everybody else's debts; whereas, if the opposite principle ruled, debtors, including the government itself, would get no relief. It has sometimes happened that, when devaluations have followed upon catastrophic depreciation, arrangements have been made to mitigate the losses of private creditors by writing up their claims in terms of the devalued money to some small extent. Even so, however, creditors are sure to suffer substantial damage for the benefit of debtors. I shall not go further into this matter. For we are interested here in the main, not in monetary catastrophes, but in the normal working of monetary systems over periods in respect of which the government's decision as to what physical entities shall be regarded as equivalent to a pound sterling — or other monetary unit — remains unchanged. For such periods the fact that this or that quantity of coined gold or a paper note inscribed in this or that way is not in itself a pound sterling, but only, in accordance with a current government proclamation, treated as equivalent to it, though legally interesting, is of no practical significance. Practically speaking, for such periods these things *are* pounds sterling; and henceforward I shall regard them as such. With this understanding, we have to frame for ourselves a definition or description of the things that we wish to count as belonging to the money system of the country.

Here a preliminary word is appropriate. It is incumbent on economists to construct their definitions in a way that is not violently discordant with common practice and at the same time, in order to avoid ambiguity, in one more precise and more uniform over different parts of the argument than is usual with such practice. These broad requirements leave considerable scope for choice and it would be idle to claim that *this* reasonably plausible definition is right and *that* wrong. Often, indeed, it may be impossible to decide even that this is more convenient than that; for the one may be more convenient for some purposes, the other for others.

It has always been agreed that, in order for anything to be classed as money, it must be accepted fairly widely as an instrument of exchange; which means that a good number of people are ready to accept it in payment for goods and services provided by them, confidently expecting that they in turn will be able to use it without troublesome delay or formality in purchasing goods or services from other people. This obviously rules out such things as houses, or elephants, or suits of clothes, or quickly perishable things like cakes or strawberries. But it does not rule out Bearer bonds or, in appropriate circumstances, cowrie shells or cigarettes. If in any society such things as these are widely used as media for exchange and recognised as such, they are *eligible to be classed* as money. But to decide which of them in any given set of conditions we should in fact so class is a delicate problem.

I shall not try to tackle this problem in a general way or to enter into legal subtleties after the manner of Knapp in his *State Theory of Money*. For our present purpose attention may be confined to modern communities, with special reference to this country. Broadly then we may say, in close agreement with common usage, that money consists of two divisions, current money and bank money. Current money (currency) for this country is substantially equivalent to all money the delivery of which is treated by the courts, in respect of some quantities and for some purposes, as a final discharge of obligations expressed in money, whether to the State or to private persons. Thus it includes gold coins, token coins and Bank of England notes, the distinction, which at one time existed, between currency notes, as obligations of the Treasury, and these notes having now disappeared. Bank money consists of bank balances — the distinction between balances on current and on deposit account is more formal than real — *plus* overdraft facilities. The notes of banks other than the Central Bank might be classed under either of these two heads, convenience favouring the former, logic perhaps the latter. But these notes now play so small a part in our monetary system that we need not trouble about them. Cheques, of course, from this point of view, are not money; they are tickets used for arranging the transfer of money from one person to another. Nor are postal orders, bills of exchange, Treasury bills or Bearer bonds of any kind money.

Within each of our two divisions money in existence must be distinguished from money in circulation. This latter includes that part of money in existence which is held outside the banking system, whether by private persons, public authorities (including the Post Office Savings Bank) or any other institution. Thus bank notes held inside the Bank of England or in the tills of the commercial banks are not money in circulation, nor are balances held by one commercial bank in another or in the Bank of England. It is thus evident that the stock of money in circulation will be enlarged if already existing currency held inside the banking system is passed into circulation no less than if new currency is created and so passed — provided, of course, that the stock of bank money in circulation is unaltered. If currency is passed into circulation by a man drawing out 100 pound notes against a cheque, the payment of which reduces by an equal amount bank money in circulation, aggregate money, *i.e.* currency *plus* bank money, in circulation is not affected.

CHAPTER II

CURRENCY AND BANK MONEY
IN GREAT BRITAIN

DIFFERENT countries have, of course, different monetary structures. It would be a lengthy and not very profitable task to describe all of these. I shall concentrate attention upon the British system. As we saw in the last chapter, the stock of money is made up of two parts, currency and bank money. These two parts are sharply distinguished from one another. It is important, however, to realise that the quantities in which they respectively circulate are not independent. In this country they are intimately linked together by two facts. First, persons and institutions outside the banks find it convenient in given circumstances to maintain some fairly definite proportion between their holdings of currency and of bank money. What this proportion is depends partly on how large a share of the money income of the country accrues to people who keep banking accounts. People without such accounts — and this includes practically all weekly wage-earners — necessarily hold the whole of their stock of money in currency. Moreover, people who have to make payments to them have, in general, to use cash for doing this. Partly again it depends on how far those people who do keep banking accounts are accustomed to pay their accounts with shops periodically on monthly bills (or advance deposits) or over the counter ; in the former case payment will generally be made by the transfer of balances through cheques, in the latter with currency.

What is customary in these matters depends on a number of factors. The development of branch banking, for example, was intended to, and did, lead to a substantial increase in the number of people who kept banking accounts. Hence the proportion in which people desire to hold currency and bank balances is by no means a constant one. Still at any given time it is settled by influences of the sort just set out. Secondly, the banks are under a legal obligation to convert balances on current account — and practically they usually treat balances on deposit account in the same way — into cash on demand ; while they will, of course, always convert cash into balances. This entails that the proportion in which people desire to hold their money in the form of currency and of balances respectively is also the proportion in which they actually do hold it in these two forms. When some accident brings about a change in the quantity of money of either sort in circulation a little time will, indeed, elapse before the customary proportion reasserts itself ; but, so long as the dominant influences governing that proportion are unaltered, it is not likely that the time-lag will be long.[1]

In theory it might quite well happen that changes in the quantity of money in circulation were initiated from the side of currency. Thus a government, wishful to purchase more services and goods than usual, might have notes printed and use them to buy what it wanted in the market. But in practice, so far as this country is concerned, that is never done. The initiative always

---

[1] The excess of the proportions in which currency, as compared with bank deposits, increased during each of the two world wars does not really throw doubt on this general relationship. It was to be expected that in periods of such large disturbance, with available income (after the payment of taxes) shifted markedly in favour of persons not likely to have banking accounts, the proportion of money held by the public in notes, as against balances, would be substantially increased.

B

comes from the side of bank money, not from the side of currency, in circulation. Even under the gold standard this was so ; for the gold that entered the Bank of England through sales of bullion only passed into circulation (or allowed notes to pass into circulation) after it had led to enlarged bank balances. Under the arrangements now ruling the same thing is true. Additions to the stock of notes in circulation are always consequential upon additions to the stock of bank balances in circulation.

When the stock of bank money in circulation is expanded the tendency towards holding a given proportion between currency in circulation and bank money in circulation will manifest itself in currency so far held inside the banking system being drawn into circulation. If the quantity of currency in existence is given, this can only be accomplished either through a reduction in the cash held by bankers in their tills or by their exchanging some of their balances at the Bank of England against notes held there and paying out to the public the notes so obtained. In either case their ' cash and balances at the Bank of England ' and the balances of the public with them are reduced by equal absolute amounts. This implies that the *proportion* of their ' cash and balances at the Bank of England ' to the balances held with them is reduced. In this country, however, convention is strongly opposed to any substantial variation in this proportion. Consequently, if the stock of currency in existence is fixed, the banks will be under pressure to prevent — whether by raising money rates, by applying severer tests of credit worthiness or otherwise — the stock of bank money in circulation from expanding by more than a certain amount. The extent of this pressure appears, if we judge from published statistics, to be very great. The clearing banks' proportion of cash and balances at the Bank of

England to deposits have seemingly been held rigid at 10 per cent for long periods together. This rigidity has, indeed, been largely a matter of window dressing, the true proportion having varied much more than the apparent one.[1] Still pressure has been real and persistent. If, however, the stock of currency in existence can be increased, the banks are under no such pressure. Large expansions under our present monetary arrangements thus entail willingness on the part of the government, whether acting through the Treasury or the Bank of England, to allow large increases in the stock of currency in existence. In the two world wars our government allowed this to any extent that might be necessary to sustain the great expansion in bank balances (in circulation) that was required to finance war expenditure.

So far of expansions in the stock of money in circulation — variations upwards. What of variations downwards? Under the gold standard, apart from possible withdrawals for use in the arts, the stock of currency in existence could only be reduced through gold being drained abroad. In this way temporary fluctuations might happen; but, while the world's gold mines continue to work, there must obviously be a general trend towards an increase in the stock of currency in existence in any gold-standard country; and, apart from special restrictive

[1] The window-dressing appearance of a highly stable proportion " has been achieved either by arranging holdings of short time governed debt to mature on the make-up date, while postponing replacements until the following day, or by calling in short term loans granted to the money market. But in either case the effect has been the same ; most of the difference between true bank cash and cash shown in the published statement has had to be created by the Bank of England. . . . Thus the true cash ratio has at times dropped to a little over 7 per cent " (*Economist*, September 7, 1946, pp. 384-5). There is reason to believe that some modification of these practices is now taking place. The conventional figure seems to be becoming set at about 8 per cent.

measures, the stock in circulation might be expected to grow more or less in proportion to the stock in existence. Bank money too, apart from changes in conventions about reserves, might be expected to move upwards along with currency; so that, on the average and in the long run, the total stock of money in circulation here would expand with the unearthing of the world's gold content; the degree of expansion being limited by the physical conditions of gold mining. There would thus be no (continuing) variation downward.

Under a pure paper currency it might be thought at first glance that notes once in existence, except for loss and wear and tear, would be as permanent as gold. But this is not so. Under the rules prevailing in this country a paper note that enters the Bank of England by that act commits suicide. It can never be reissued, but is destroyed. This, however, is a secondary matter. Notes will not re-enter the Bank of England in the ordinary course unless there is a net repayment of loans that have been made by banks to the public or to public authorities. Unless a deliberate policy of deflation is adopted, taxes or loans being raised from the public and used to cancel debts to the banks, there will not be such a net repayment. For, many wage rates and salaries having adapted themselves to the increased stock of money in circulation, there will be no reason, on the average of good and bad times, for the public (as distinguished from the government) to try to repay them. In fact the expansion in bank deposits and also in currency, which took place during the course of the first world war, was not cancelled subsequently; nor is there any likelihood that the expansion associated with the second war will fare differently. Contractions in *money income* may, indeed, easily occur — witness industrial depressions generally and, in particular, the great slump of the early 1930's. But they are almost always and almost entirely brought about by way of reductions in the frequency with which the representative unit of circulating money appears as money income, that is to say, in its income velocity, not by contractions in the stock of money in circulation.

CHAPTER III

THE MEANING OF INFLATION

IN this book I shall use the term inflation, not, as is sometimes done, in relation to the stock of money or of currency in existence or in circulation, but in relation to the size of a country's aggregate money income. This money income is liable from time to time to expand or contract. We might, if we chose, use inflation to mean an expansion and deflation to mean a contraction of it. But that would be a waste of words. I shall say that inflation is taking place when money income is expanding relatively to the output of work — not the output of goods and services (real income) — by productive agents, for which it is the payment; and that in opposite conditions deflation is taking place. Thus there is no inflation when an expansion of money income is associated, whether as consequence or as cause, with an equi-proportionate expansion in the quantity of productive resources at work. Nor does it matter whether the extra work comes from an increase in these resources or from the employment of a larger proportion of those that already exist.

According to this definition inflation may be taking place even though money income is contracting, provided that output of work by men and machines is contracting in a larger proportion. This is out of line with common speech, which always, in a vague way, associates inflation with expansion. To that extent my definition has a paradoxical sound. In periods of full-scale war inflation of a non-expansionary type does not occur. For such times, therefore, the fact that it is included in the above definition does not much matter. But in times of peace it creates an awkwardness. Further, on that definition inflation occurs when money income expands more than in proportion to the work of productive agents, not when it expands more than in proportion to the real income of services and goods passing to the final buyer. Hence, when the volume of resources employed is given, inflation is necessarily associated with a rise in the rates of pay to productive agents, but not necessarily with a rise in the prices of services and goods received by final buyers. If, through technical improvements and so on, the productivity of these agents is increasing fast enough, inflation may be taking place even though prices are falling. In the same way, if the productivity of these agents is declining fast enough, deflation may be taking place in company with rising prices. Thus again, from the standpoint of common usage, my definition is paradoxical. Once more in periods of full-scale war the paradox does not matter, because it is practically certain that productive efficiency will not, in fact, increase fast enough to make prices fall; but for times of peace it does.

In spite of these paradoxes I am inclined to hold to my definition. When, however, we attempt to measure inflation so defined, we cannot hope for more than a very partial success. Money income being a single homogeneous thing, the proportion in which the quantity of it varies between any two years is, indeed, unambiguous — so much per cent; and, though, of course, there may be practical difficulties in the way, it is in principle susceptible of precise measurement. But productive agents are not homogeneous; there are a variety of different sorts of agent. Unless, therefore, by a miracle, the outputs of work

by all of them (roughly the quantity of hours' work done
by all of them) vary in the same proportion, the proportion in which the work of these agents as a whole varies is
not an unambiguous physical magnitude. Attempts to
measure variations in it, and, therefore, also in inflation
as here defined, are thus subject to the same difficulty
that, as we shall find in Chapter IX, hinders the measurement of the purchasing power of a pound or of aggregate
money income. There is, however, a partial way out. On
the assumption that the other factors at work have varied
in quantity in the same proportion as the number of wage-
earners employed, inflation in my sense as between two
periods will be correctly measured by

$$\frac{\text{money income in year 2}}{\text{money income in year 1}} \div \frac{\text{employment in year 2}}{\text{employment in year 1}}.$$

For this purpose, the proportionate changes in employment must be so reckoned as to allow for changes in the
hours of work, *i.e.* by the proportionate change in employment as ordinarily reckoned multiplied by the proportionate
change in the length of the working day. Allowance
ought also to be made for any variations that may have
taken place in the work power of the average worker
consequent either on improvements in nutrition or in
training or on shifts in the proportion of women and
children in the labour force. *What* allowance should be
made under these heads between given dates can only be
settled by that kind of guesswork which is usually called
' judgement '. In actual life, in respect of short-period
fluctuations, it is probable that the quantity of labour at
work varies more than the quantity of capital equipment,
but over a long period in current conditions the quantity
of equipment almost certainly rises faster. Therefore,
the above measure of inflation probably under-estimates

the amount of it for short-run and over-estimates it for long-run expansions. During a short period of full-scale war the quantities of labour and of equipment at work are probably both nearly stationary; so that our measure reduces to $\dfrac{\text{money income of year 2}}{\text{money income of year 1}}$. Over the course of such a period (*e.g.* 1944–5) variations in the average rate of money wages for persons of a given degree of skill working for a given length of working day would not give bad measure of inflation and deflation in the senses in which I use those terms.

CHAPTER IV

MONEY, A VEIL?

IN the years preceding the first world war there were in common use among economists a number of metaphors, all of a like general tendency, about the rôle of money. ' Money is a wrapper in which goods come to you ' ; ' money is the garment draped round the body of economic life ' ; ' money is a veil behind which the action of real economic forces is concealed '. The mercantilists, it was said, in their blindness, mistook money for wealth ; we must not do that. We must strip off the garment, tear away the veil, look through the thing to the thing signified. Nor was this merely precept. In one important department of economics at least, international trade, analysis was conducted in terms of linen bartered against cloth, or bales of exports against bales of imports, money being brought in only after the main work was done. J. S. Nicholson did, indeed, try to get at things from the opposite end, but the old way — Ricardo's way — was dominant. In the first world war, Lloyd George's silver bullets notwithstanding, man-power, equipment and organisation became more and more, and money less and less, central in economic thought. With the violent disturbances in prices and exchange rates throughout the world in the earlier years of peace, the enforced abandonment of the gold standard by this country in 1925, and the great slump of the early 1930's, money, the passive veil, took on the appearance of an active and evil genius ; the garment became a Nessus shirt ; the wrapper a thing liable to explode. Money, in short, after being little or nothing, was now everything; liquidity preference and the balance of money payments the small change of economic discussion. Then, with the second world war, the tune changed again. Man-power, equipment and organisation once more came into their own. The rôle of money dwindled to insignificance. It was now not even a veil, but, in the language of a not unimportant politician, no better than a ' meaningless symbol '.

To laymen these variations of language and emphasis may seem discreditable to economists and, if I may so describe the general body of politicians and political publicists, near-economists. But that is hardly fair. For in truth the part played by money is much more important in some situations than it is in others, and it is natural that in these different situations current economic analysis should be focussed, and its emphasis adjusted, accordingly. It is not discreditable to doctors and nurses that their customary language, the tone of their thought and the proportions of their emphasis differ in periods dominated by different types of epidemic or endemic disease. There is no call, therefore, for an apology. But there is a call for some attempt to co-ordinate our ideas on these matters and see things in the round.

In the deepest sense economic reality comprises states of mind — the satisfactions and dissatisfactions of human beings — and nothing else. Battleships, tomatoes, concerts, are in themselves of no significance whatever. What is significant about them is the fact that people directly or indirectly get enjoyment or other sorts of satisfaction out of them and suffer, or may suffer, dis-enjoyment or dissatisfaction in the process of producing them. States of mind are the things in which economists are ultimately interested. But the main part of their work does not penetrate to these depths. It is concerned with a subordinate reality ancillary to the ultimate one, material goods and immaterial services, the ' necessaries and conveniences of life ', as they are on the one hand consumed or held, on the other produced : and in the stocks of labour-power, capital and natural resources, out of which production flows. This complex whole and the movements of its interrelated parts constitute the reality that economists have in mind when they distinguish, as they often do, between ' real ' and monetary facts and processes.

To every community there are available at any time certain resources provided by Nature, which the classical economists compendiously called Land ; a certain accumulation of objects made by man, with the help perhaps of other like objects, called Capital ; and a certain population of men, women and children endowed with various types of skill. Out of this population the workers, brain workers and hand workers together, or rather those of them who are at the time employed, co-operate with Land and Capital to produce a great variety of goods and direct services, including, as a rule, some net addition to the stock of capital. This inventory of objects is commonly called the community's ' real income '. If the community is in contact with other communities a part of the process of production may be indirect, our community producing one set of things to be exchanged with other communities for another set, which then enters, while the things exchanged away do not enter, into its real income. All the things entering into that real income are distributed among the members of our community in one way or another. The amount of work that people do, the way in which this work is allocated among different occupations, between the production of consumer's goods and of capital

goods and among the various kinds of each, the amount
and kinds of the goods and services that result, and the
variations in all these elements that take place from time
to time, are for the economist the essential things and the
primary object of his study.

One aspect of this reality can be displayed by way of
an instantaneous photograph. In such a photograph no
indication will appear of any process of movement. The
picture will comprise, not flows at all, only stocks. Thus
there will be seen, in part rooted to the ground, such-and-
such a physical equipment of fixed capital, including
houses, such-and-such stocks of raw materials, of partly
grown crops and partly manufactured goods, standing in
what has been called the machine of process ; such-and-
such stocks of physically finished goods standing in what
we may call the machine of distribution, *i.e.* in the hands
of wholesalers, transporting agents and retail dealers ;
such-and-such stocks of completed goods, including
motor-cars and other forms of consumer's capital, standing
in people's homes ; and, lastly, such-and-such a stock of
human beings of various ages and capacity.

An instantaneous picture is, however, of much less
interest than a moving one ; because the wheel of our
economy is not at rest, but in continuous revolution. The
term ' stationary state ', as used by economists, is, indeed,
not linguistically apt. The idea that it was meant to
convey is not, as the word suggests, that of non-motion
but that of rotation at a constant speed, neither accelerating
nor decelerating. Consider then an economy in a stationary
state in that sense, or, what comes to the same thing, in
any state restricted to a time interval short enough to
allow such accelerations or decelerations as may be taking
place to be ignored. In a moving picture of this all the
several stocks described in the last paragraph remain

constant in size. No additions to or subtractions from
any of them take place; which implies that there is no
net investment or disinvestment, and no change in the
size of the population of working age. The shape of the
waterfall is unvarying, but the place occupied at one
moment by this drop is, the next moment, occupied by
that one. Parts of the stock of fixed capital are continuously being worn out and replaced. Raw materials
and partly manufactured goods move continuously forward through the machine of process, passing into the
machine of distribution and, through that again, into the
hands of the final holders; corresponding quantities of
material being fed into the machine of process by an intake
pipe and worked up inside in such wise as exactly to
balance the outflow. Of what flows to the final holders
a part replaces wear and tear of consumer's capital —
motor-cars, furniture, clothes, crockery and so on —; a
part, after a momentary stay in larders and kitchens, is
literally consumed in the bodies of the people; a part,
such as the services rendered by doctors, teachers and
musicians, passes directly into consumption without any
mediating machine.

The final holders, to whom all these goods flow out,
are all the time, with the help of the stock of capital equipment, performing the work by means of which new
materials are continuously pushed through the intake
pipe into the machine of process and operated upon inside
it. The goods which finally emerge in any time interval
are the result of efforts scattered over a prior period, the
centre of gravity of which, so to speak, stands, for each
sort of good, a specifiable number of days backward in
time. For all sorts of goods that enter into real income
taken together this number of days must obviously bear
to 365 the same ratio that the stock of goods in process

and distribution — working capital — bears to annual income. For this country there is reason to believe that the ratio is in the neighbourhood of one-half. That, however, from the present standpoint, is a secondary matter. The essential fact, to put it paradoxically, is that our economic machine is a perpetual motion machine, whose movement generates the fuel which keeps the movement going.

Thus far of the so-called stationary state. But in actual life the wheel does not rotate at constant velocity, the waterfall does not retain a constant shape or size. If, instead of restricting ourselves to a very short length of moving-picture reel, we run through a moderately long one, this becomes at once apparent. The several stocks we have distinguished change in volume and in the form of their content from time to time. We might imagine for ourselves if we wished — and for some purposes this would prove a convenient imagining — an economy growing continuously in all its parts at one and the same constant geometrical rate.[1] In actual life we do not find economies moving in steady progress of any sort ; but, rather, successive curlings and uncurlings, after the manner of a caterpillar. The waterfall may on the whole be increasing (or decreasing) in size ; but in some time intervals of given length the increase is much larger than in others, while in some there may be actual decreases. Moreover, the shape of the waterfall neither remains

---

[1] It would be impossible for all its parts to grow at the same constant *arithmetical* rate. For, if the flow of consumption goods is to increase at a constant arithmetical rate, the stock of equipment must (on obviously plausible assumptions) increase at that constant arithmetical rate ; and this implies that, apart from the need for replacements, the output of the industries making equipment is not increasing at all. It should be noted that there is no general *a priori* reason for believing it to be possible for all the parts of a whole to increase even at one and the same *geometrical* rate. If a pet elephant this year contains twice the volume of flesh and bone that it did last, it will contain much less than twice the area of skin.

constant nor varies in a constant manner ; while the drops that were originally water alter from time to time, consisting now perhaps of wine, now of vinegar. The total outflow of goods and services, the types of these, the total quantity of work-people finding employment, their various qualities, the total quantity of equipment at work and its various kinds, all these things continuously shift and change ; and all the shifts and changes our long strip of film faithfully records.

Over against the real facts and happenings thus roughly outlined there stand monetary facts and happenings. There is not, indeed, any *a priori* necessity about this. In primitive conditions small groups of neighbours, or even families, were in great part self-sufficing. A farm family grew its own food, made its own clothes, kept its own house in repair. A substantial part of the work that a man did and of the services that he rendered yielded their product directly to himself. Now, however, in the main for nearly everybody this is not so. With the division of labour carried so far as it has been it could not be so. In general, what a man receives as real income consists only to a very small extent of things to the production of which his own particular work has contributed. By far the predominant part he obtains by exchanging, and exchanging against money, so that money income, which is the obverse of money expenditure by final buyers — not, of course, by intermediaries — is the purchase price, or value, of the community's real income. It is in connection with this exchanging that monetary facts and happenings come into being. They differ from ' real ' facts and happenings in that, unlike these, they have no *direct* significance for economic welfare. Take the real facts and happenings away, and the monetary facts and happenings necessarily vanish with them ; but take money away and, whatever else might follow, economic life would *not* become meaningless: there is nothing absurd about the conception of a self-sufficing family, or village group, without any money at all. In this sense money clearly *is* a veil. It does not comprise any of the essentials of economic life.

But this is not to say that monetary facts and happenings are unimportant to economic life. The body is more than raiment; but, none the less, raiment greatly affects the comfort of the body. Thus money — the institution of money — is an extremely valuable social instrument, making a large contribution to economic welfare. Under any conditions other than the most primitive, people find it, as we have seen, economically advantageous to carry on a great deal of interchange among various sorts of goods and services. Such interchange by way of direct barter, if not entirely impracticable, would, as is abundantly illustrated in the text-books, be extremely inconvenient and costly in time and trouble; so much so that, if there were no generally accepted money, many of these transactions would not be worth undertaking, and, as a direct consequence, the division of labour would be hampered and less services and goods would be produced. Thus not only would real income be allocated less satisfactorily, from the standpoint of economic welfare, among different sorts of goods, but it would also contain smaller amounts of many, if not of all sorts. Obviously then money is not *merely* a veil or a garment or a wrapper. Like the laws of property and contract, it constitutes at the least a very useful lubricant, enabling the economic machine to function continuously and smoothly; a railway through the air, the loss of which would inflict on us the same sort of damage as we should suffer if the actual railways and roads, by which the different parts of the

c

country are physically linked together, were destroyed.

So far everyone would be agreed. But now an important distinction must be drawn. The *institution* of money is, as we have seen, a powerful instrument promoting wealth and welfare. But the *number of units of money* embodied in that instrument is, in general, of no significance. It is all one whether the garment, or the veil, is thick or thin. I do not mean, of course, that it is immaterial whether the number of units of money is held constant, òr is variable in one manner, or is variable in another manner in relation to other economic happenings. I mean that if, other things being equal, over a series of months or years the stock of money contains successively mx_1, mx_2, mx_3 . . . units, it makes no difference what the value of m is. A doubled value of m throughout means simply doubled prices throughout of every type of goods — subject, of course, to the rate of interest not being reckoned for this purpose as a price — ; and all real happenings are exactly what they would have been with a value of m half as large. The reason for this is that, money being only useful *because* it exchanges for other things, a larger quantity does not, as with other things, carry more satisfaction on its back than a smaller quantity, but the same satisfaction. As we are dealing in similes, a new one, to clinch this argument, may be allowed us. Money then, let us say, is a key, by means of which productive energies, that would otherwise have been imprisoned, can be released ; but, provided only it fits the lock, it is of no significance whether the key contains a great deal of metal or very little

So far everything is clear. If then we were confronted in the actual world with the steadily rotating state, inaptly called stationary, of economic fiction, there would be no further question to ask and nothing more to say. But the fact of change destroys this convenient simplicity. The economic body alters, and the veil that shrouds, or the garment that enwraps it, alters also. How are these alterations related ? At one time it was the practice of an important school of writers to assert that psychical happenings were mere epiphenomena of physical happenings ; that they were wholly an effect of these latter happenings and in no degree reacted upon them. Pressure on the heart caused mental distress, but mental distress could not cause pressure on the heart ; laughter caused pleasurable emotion, not, as the layman might suppose, pleasurable emotion laughter. In like manner, it might be argued, all changes which occur in the money garment result from changes initiated in the body, and these changes in the garment do not react in any way on the body ; just as, if the number of persons travelling in a railway train were recorded by an enterprising spy, the record would be a mere epiphenomenon. The similes of the garment, the veil and the wrapper suggest that this is in fact so. But the suggestion is wrong. Many important changes that occur in the garment are, indeed, effects of changes initiated in the body. But, in general, these in turn react in a greater or less degree on the state of the body. *What* changes in the garment result from given changes initiated in the body and what reactions they, or the lack of them, in turn produce depends on how the garment is constructed. Besides these induced changes that occur in the garment there are, or may be, other changes that are autonomous, originating in the garment itself. These too have effects on the body. What they are and what their effects again depends on how the garment is constructed.

CHAPTER V

THE PRICE SYSTEM AND THE
DISTRIBUTION OF SUPPLIES

THE institution of money enables every sort of article and service to be docketed with a value ticket expressed in terms of a single thing. This arrangement plays an important part both as regards the distribution of each several kind of saleable thing among the people who want it and as regards the allocation of productive resources to the provision of different sorts of things. These two aspects of the price system will be discussed in this and the following chapter. In this one I shall examine the distribution aspect.

The supplies of anything, that flow out of the machine of process, have to be distributed somehow among the people who want them. There are a number of alternative ways in which this can be done. The way to which we are or, rather, used to be accustomed in peace-time is that of a market in which prices and the purchases made by individuals are unhampered by any kind of government intervention. In these conditions, the sellers are led to put prices at such a level that the quantity of their product demanded is equal to the quantity supplied. Ideally, therefore, apart from accidents and friction, nobody, who, at the price ruling, wants to obtain any of them, is unable to do so. This result is achieved because the price is put at the level which restricts the demands of would-be purchasers in the degree that allows it to be achieved. If all incomes and all tastes were alike, the quantities of

anything demanded by and so distributed to each pur-
chaser would be the same. As things are, among people
of equal incomes more coffee is distributed to people
who like it more relatively to tea and less to people who
like it less ; and, among people of similar tastes, more is
distributed to those with larger than to those with smaller
incomes. Thus the price system serves as an instrument
enabling the available supplies of each several sort of
commodity or service to be distributed among the public
in accordance with the combined pressures of their incomes
and their tastes. All demands — not, of course, all
desires — are exactly satisfied. Given his income and the
price situation, every consumer has complete freedom of
choice.

This way of distribution entails, since money income
is a determinant of demand, that better-to-do people in
general obtain a larger share per head of the available
supply of any ordinary commodity than poor people do.
There are exceptions to this rule. Thus bread and other
very cheap articles of food may be consumed in larger
quantities by a representative poor man than by a representative rich man, because the rich man can afford
to buy more costly alternative foods and the poor man
cannot. But for most things the rule holds. If it is felt
that the rich are getting too large a share of the national
output on account of their large incomes, it is open to the
State to cut into these, directly by heavily graduated income
and surtax, and indirectly by heavily graduated death
duties ; the proceeds being transferred to the poor. If
there is some special kind of commodity, such as housing
accommodation or, perhaps, milk, of which, on medical
or other grounds, it is thought desirable that poor people
should consume more than the free play of the market
will allow them to do, it can be purchased by the State

out of tax revenue and directly handed over gratis in quantities judged appropriate to each separate individual ; as with teaching and milk for school children under the Education Acts. Alternatively, subsidies can be paid by the Treasury either on the production of that commodity as a whole or on the purchases of it made by defined categories of poor persons. In either case the poor as a consequence would get more absolutely ; in the latter certainly, in the former probably, more proportionately also. But none of these arrangements — positive quantity controls as we may call them — nor yet any system of priorities unaccompanied by price regulation for non-priority buyers, would interfere at all with the normal working of the price system. Different ingredients would be put into the machine and the output from it would be correspondingly different. But the functioning of the machine would be unaffected. It would still secure that all demands were exactly satisfied ; that no demander at the ruling price would be unable to obtain that quantity of stuff which at that price he was demanding.

There are, however, two sorts of State interference which, if adopted, do prevent all demands from being exactly satisfied. The first consists in rules that preclude some people from buying as much of some commodity as they wish, either by the imposition of uniform *ration limits* — this does not, of course, entail uniform *rations* — or through a system of licencing, under which different people's purchases are restricted in different degrees according to the purpose to which they propose to put the purchased article. For a few commodities, in particular noxious or dangerous drugs, negative quantity controls of this kind may be imposed with a view to cutting down total consumption. But in general the intention is to restrict consumption by some persons or for some purposes in order that more of the commodity may be available for others. This was the intention behind the great body of war-time restrictions upon purchases. Owing to the diversion of a large part of the country's energies to fighting, munition-making and various forms of defence, the volume of goods and services available for ordinary civilian use was very much cut down ; those goods which have to be imported from abroad being affected, because of the damage done by war to foreign trade, in an especially high degree. In these circumstances, as also, of course, in such abnormal peace-time but war-affected conditions as have recently prevailed, to allow distribution to be settled by the free play of the market is bound to mean that the demand of better-to-do persons will force up prices beyond what poorer persons can afford, so that the main burden of the shortage is concentrated upon them. It is as though the depleted stores of a besieged city were shared out between the physically strong and the physically weak by ordeal of rough and tumble. This is intolerable. The government is bound to seek something better ; and the way out that naturally suggests itself is to restrict the amount of purchases permitted to better-to-do persons or for relatively non-urgent purposes. This inevitably means that some demands are not satisfied.

The second sort of State interference that may prevent all demands from being satisfied is the fixing of effective maximum prices, *i.e.* maximum prices higher than would rule if, other things being the same, no maximum was fixed. Here, however, there is a complication. In the case of goods produced under conditions of monopoly, if an effective maximum price is fixed intermediate between the monopoly price and what we may call the appropriate competitive price, the quantity demanded will be enhanced. But, since restriction of output cannot enable the monopolist to lift prices against consumers above the decreed maximum price, the quantity supplied will also be enhanced. This second enhancement will in some circumstances be as large as, in others smaller than the first enhancement. The chance that it will be as large is *pro tanto* stronger (1) if the demand for the commodity over the relevant range is inelastic and (2) if the decreed price is only a little less than what the monopolist would have chosen to charge if left to his own devices. The reader interested in analysis may find entertainment in proving this.[1] Obviously, when the effect of fixing an effective maximum price is to make supply expand as much as demand, all demands are satisfied, just as they would be if there were no maximum price. For monopolised commodities, therefore, it is only in *some* circumstances that the fixing of maximum prices interferes with the normal tendency of the price system to secure this result. With commodities produced under conditions of competition there is no such uncertainty. The fixing of a maximum price below the competitive price is bound to enhance the quantity demanded, and cannot cause the quantity supplied to increase.[2] Therefore, it *must* prevent the price mechanism from securing that all demands are satisfied.

The fixing of maximum prices for monopolised commodities is a matter of general social policy, dependent on wider considerations than can suitably be discussed here. I shall, therefore, confine attention to price restriction in conditions of competition, or, more generally, where the ground for restriction is not defence against

---

[1] Cf. *The Economics of Welfare*, 4th edition, p. 809.

[2] When a commodity is said to be produced under conditions of increasing returns this means, of course, that an enlarged scale of output, appropriate adjustments having been made, causes price to be lower, *not* that a lower price causes the scale of output to be larger.

monopoly. This is not the sort of policy that any government will adopt — unless, of course, it makes its official price a competitive one by paying an appropriate subsidy — in normal times. For, if it fixed the price too low, it would destroy, and, in any event, it would reduce, output ; and, if it wanted to do that, it could always do it by imposing a tax. But on special occasions, when part of the normal sources of supply of some article have been cut off, for example, by war, those suppliers, who are fortunate enough to continue in being, will confront a competitive price much higher than the old one, which, if they are allowed to charge it, will yield them enormous profits. In these circumstances the government could, if it chose, leave prices alone and, nevertheless, deprive these people of their windfalls by a full-scale excess profits tax. But this would be little comfort to the particular groups of consumers who had had to pay these abnormal prices. Consequently, the government may well prefer, as an alternative or complementary policy, to fix maximum prices. It must be careful, of course, not to fix them at a level that will dry up the sources of supply. Eggs will not be produced if people are not allowed to sell them at prices high enough to cover the cost of feeding stuffs for their hens. Particularly with things imported from abroad, unless foreign prices *plus* cost of transport are covered (or any gap that emerges made good by a subsidy), the imports will not come. But in the conditions of which we are now thinking there is usually a wide margin between the scarcity competitive price and a price low enough to destroy, or even sensibly to diminish, the volume of supplies coming on to the market ; and anywhere inside this gap the government can safely decree a maximum price.

So far, then, the fixing of maximum ration limits (and

analogous devices) and the fixing of effective maximum prices, in some circumstances under monopoly, in all circumstances under competition, are liable to obstruct the working of the price mechanism in similar ways. There is, however, a very important difference. Rationing and similar devices prevent some demands from being satisfied. They accomplish this by establishing a distinction between permitted demands and other demands. Under them all permitted demands are satisfied. Consequently, distribution is orderly. There are no queues ; nor is there any other obvious call for further sorts of interference to take care of difficulties created by this sort of interference. This sort in fact can, if need be, stand secure on its own legs. With price control that is not so. As with rationing so here, alongside of demands that are satisfied there are a number of unsatisfied ghosts. As with rationing too how many of these there shall be is determined by the level at which it is decided to set the maximum price, in conjunction with the general conditions of demand. But *what particular demands* are to become ghosts, *which* would-be purchasers are to leave the market empty-handed, is not in this case settled in an orderly way. If nothing further is done beyond fixing a maximum price, who succeed in getting and who fail to get what they want depends on accident, favouritism by shopkeepers, ability to bring to bear on them one or another kind of pressure, the leisure and the capacity to stand without fainting for a long period in a queue. This sort of distribution not only entails for many people waste of time, worry and a sense of grievance, but, at all events for the sorts of goods which satisfy elementary needs, is a serious social danger.

To obviate these things, when the State decides to fix maximum prices for essential articles — with non-essential articles the disadvantages of chaos in distribution are smaller and the administrative difficulty of preventing them is larger — it frequently at the same time fixes maximum individual rations so contrived as to keep the aggregate amount of the commodity that people desire *and are allowed* to buy down to the level of the aggregate supply. Thus price control and rationing are both introduced together. With that arrangement some demands are still, as before, not satisfied, but the social disorganisation, which, apart from the addition of rationing, might have resulted from price control, is held at bay.

We conclude then broadly that, if in respect of any commodity the State does not interfere either by effective rationing (or something equivalent) or by fixing effective maximum prices, all demands will be exactly satisfied through the price system. If effective rationing is established this will not happen. If effective price maxima are fixed, it *may* not happen under monopoly and *will* not happen under conditions of competition. If maximum prices are imposed without rationing (or something equivalent), in cases where the maximum price prevents some demands from being satisfied, distribution is not orderly, but depends on chance or favouritism. But by superimposing on any given maximum-price arrangement an appropriate system of rationing, *i.e.* one that cuts down permitted demand to equality with supply, the State can overcome this disorder. It prevents the price system from doing its job, but it provides a (more or less) satisfactory substitute.[1]

---

[1] Cf. *post*, Note to Part I, Chap. V, pp. 148-9.

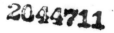

CHAPTER VI

THE PRICE SYSTEM AND THE
ALLOCATION OF PRODUCTIVE RESOURCES

BESIDES acting as a mechanism for the distribution of
each particular commodity among the people who want
it, the price system also provides one for allocating productive resources among different uses. The way in which,
in the absence of State intervention, this mechanism works
is well understood. If firms engaged in making a particular kind of commodity find that, at the ruling price,
they are getting bigger returns on the money they lay
out than are being got elsewhere, they are under inducement to take on more capital and labour, bidding for
additional supplies in the market. Maybe this action of
theirs enables lenders to get a slight rise of interest and
work-people in their service to get rather higher wages.
In any event, ordinary shareholders who put their money
into this industry can look for better returns, and work-
people engaged there for a fuller measure of employment.
Consequently, resources are attracted into the industry
that makes the commodity affected, and the attraction
continues to work until, with increased output and lowered
price, the prospects from engagement there are no longer
better than the prospects elsewhere. Thus influences
acting through the price system are continually tending to
bring about such an allocation of resources among different
kinds of production that the value of the yield of each sort
of resource — strictly of the marginal yield of each sort —
is the same for all of them. This tendency is, of course,

seriously distorted by monopolistic practice in various guises and degrees; so that, even if the economic system remained in a stationary state for a long period, it would never work itself out completely. Moreover, in practice all sorts of disturbing factors are continually intervening. The pursuer never actually catches the pursued, but he is always chasing after him; and in the process of this chasing is adjusting the allocation of resources among different uses as nearly as he can so as to make the values of the marginal private returns to them (subject to monopolistic distortions) everywhere equal.

This pattern of allocation is not, of course, to be regarded as in any sense ideal. The so-called doctrine of maximum satisfaction is ruined by the facts (1) that, as observed above, entry into certain occupations is hindered by monopolistic practices, whether operated by employers or by trade unions, (2) that in some occupations there is a return of benefit or of damage spilling over, as it were, from the persons directly concerned to other people who have no part in determining the allocation, and (3) that a pound's worth of demand by a rich man is almost certainly associated with much less satisfaction than a pound's worth by a poor man. In view of these facts there is a strong *prima facie* case for State action through taxes and bounties to encourage some and discourage other sorts of expenditure and to modify the 'natural' allocation of productive resources.

All this, however, has nothing to do with the mechanism of the price system. For, as was indicated in the last chapter, anything that the State may do by way of fiscal devices leaves that mechanism intact. When, however, either a maximum permitted ration or a maximum price for anything is fixed for the sake, maybe, of fairness between better- and worse-off candidates for purchasing that thing, the mechanism itself, not merely the conditions in which it is working, is disrupted. Labour and capital are then discouraged from moving over to the production of things that have been subjected to maximum ration limits or, except in some circumstances under monopoly, to price restriction. But this is not the only or the principal way in which the price mechanism, as an instrument for allocating resources among different uses, may be disrupted. It is disrupted also if that allocation is interfered with by decree. Thus the State may commandeer, requisition or conscribe the human or other resources that it requires, paying for them what it thinks proper but seizing them irrespective of the willingness or otherwise of their owners. This method stands at the extremest distance from the normal peace-time method of straightforward purchase in a free and undoctored market. But there are also available a number of intermediate and mixed methods. Alternatively, while a purchase price may be offered which the person to whom it is offered *need* not accept, if he does not accept coercion to something else is imposed on him; if he will not do munition work he may be called up to the army; or jobs to which he would like to move rather than stay in, say, munition-making, may be forbidden to him.

Of the motives behind rationing and price restriction for particular commodities, by which the price mechanism as an instrument for allocating resources among different uses is indirectly ruptured, enough was said in the last chapter. Why does the State also sometimes, and predominantly in time of war, interfere by direct fiat? The fundamental reason is that large shifts in the allocation of resources cannot be brought about through the price mechanism otherwise than slowly. If the economic system were stationary, that would not matter because there would not be any shifts. But in actual life it is very important.

When the demand for one kind of product or service expands relatively to that for another, adult persons trained to and engaged in the one are not easily induced to move to the other, in which, maybe, their acquired skill will have little value. In the same way people who have established themselves with their families in one place are not easily induced to move elsewhere. There is a great deal of friction to overcome; and the liberal provision now made under the Insurance Acts for persons unable to find work at their accustomed jobs inevitably weakens an ordinary man's eagerness to overcome it. In the long run the relative numbers of persons engaged in different occupations and places can be adjusted to demand changes without any shifting of occupation by people already in employment, simply by diversion from one route to another of the inflow of new recruits. But, since the new recruits who enter industry annually constitute, especially in men's industries, only a small proportion of the number engaged there, adjustment by this means cannot be rapid. In like manner, adjustment in the number of persons available for work at different places can in the long run be made by movements on the part of young people, who are able to move easily. But, here again, because these young people are only a small part of the whole population, the adjustment cannot be rapid. For these reasons, when large-scale changes in industrial organisation are needed for some overriding purpose — most obviously when peace gives place to war — the price system is not an effective instrument, and governments are inevitably led to supplement it by direct or indirect coercion.

It would, indeed, be a mistake to suppose that the slowness of the adjustments observed in ordinary life are due solely to the fact that reliance is there placed on the suasion of price. Some lapse, in a sense some waste, of time is inevitable and cannot be done away with, no matter what instrument of adjustment is employed. Thus for purely technical reasons nearly every kind of economic development must proceed by stages, and the later stages cannot be begun until earlier ones have been completed. A house must be built from the ground up, the top storey being constructed after, and not at the same time as, the one below. Thus the speed with which an army can be created is narrowly limited until sufficient instructors have been trained, and the number of aeroplanes that can be put into operation by the number of airfields available. Again, the manufacture of machines must wait on the provision of machine tools ; and an enlargement in the output of tanks and aeroplanes beyond what can be turned out from existing factories cannot take place until new factories have been built and equipped. Moreover, before the production of any hitherto untried thing can be started on a significant scale, a great deal of preliminary work must be done on design and experiment. Thus when war breaks out a great volume of labour and other resources, which everybody knows will be wanted in the war machine once it has got into its stride, cannot be used there for a considerable time. This is true of any country that is normally geared to peace, though, of course, the situation is quite different in countries where a period of nominal peace has in fact been devoted in the main to preparation for war. The consequential slowness of adjustment has nothing to do with the mechanism of the price system and cannot be done away with by substituting something else. This, however, is by the way. Nobody doubts that, in addition to delays in adjustment that are inevitable, there are also very important delays — they were described a few pages back — associated with reliance on this mechanism.

The extent of these delays depends in great part on how far, when services and equipment come to be wanted more keenly than before for particular uses, those who want them are prepared to bid prices up. For a man, who will not transfer his labour power or equipment belonging to him out of its present use to a new one for an offer 10 per cent in excess of their normal value, might well do so in response to one several hundred per cent in excess of that. This consideration is very relevant to what happens in time of war. The State, with its power to raise taxes and to create new money, has a bottomless purse ; and could, if it chose, offer enormous payments in order to divert men and equipment from other uses to war service. But it cannot make the inducement very large except at heavy current real cost to the people whose services and equipment are not specially needed and, maybe too, at the expense of serious currency dislocation ; while those who are fortunate enough to possess the personal qualities and the kinds of equipment that the State needs will make fantastic gains. For this reason, even though it *could* satisfy its requirements completely by operating through the price system and making large offers, it might well, and in fact in modern conditions it always does, prefer to rely, at least in part, on fiat. How far it does this depends on a country's traditions and customs, on the intensity of the war need, on experience as to what is practically effective and on the temper of the people — what the government thinks that they will stand without loss of morale or too loud an outcry. It is likely to be different for different countries in different wars and at different stages in the same war. What we have to do with here is political art, not economic science.

In war-time then, at least in wars on a great scale, the rôle of the price system as an instrument through play upon which the allocation of labour and equipment among rival occupations and places is achieved is, in great part, superseded. Money payments are, of course, still made for services rendered and for the use of equipment, but the payments are, it may be decreed, it may be indirectly manipulated; they are an addendum to the economic process, not a link in the causal chain which determines it. After all, however, large-scale war is — at least so we may hope — an exceptional and abnormal condition. In peace-time in the western world, as distinct from Russia, the allocation of men and equipment among occupations and places has hitherto been predominantly regulated, without direct or indirect coercion, by the ordinary forces of demand and supply acting through the price system; the State, where it intervenes at all, intervening in ways that use, and do not by-pass or nullify, that system. The introduction in this country of peace-time conscription for young men for service with the armed forces has, indeed, made a breach in that general rule; and recent legislation restricting, through exchange control, the investment of capital abroad has made another. But in relation to the economy as a whole these breaches are not of wide scope. Such others as remain are under notice to disappear. If, as there is still room for hope, most of them do in fact presently disappear, the account I gave in the earlier paragraphs of this chapter of the way in which the allocation of resources among occupations and places is regulated *through*, not, of course, *by* the price system will be broadly true of post-war, as it was of pre-war, England.

CHAPTER VII

MONEY AS AN INSTRUMENT OF
SAVING OR INVESTMENT

THE excess for any man of real income over consumption
I call his real saving, and the deficiency of real income
below consumption his real dis-saving. The real saving
of any closed group of persons is, therefore, the excess of
the real saving of those of its members who save over the
real dis-saving of those who dis-save. But real income or
output is evidently made up of aggregate real consumption
plus aggregate real investment. Hence aggregate real
saving and aggregate real investment are two names for
the same thing. Of course, the real saving of one individual in the group may be transferred to another individual and eaten up by his real dis-saving, so that the real
saving of an individual does not necessarily manifest itself
as real investment. But for the representative member of
the group it *must* do this, and it is, therefore, convenient
to focus attention upon him.

In a Robinson Crusoe economy, if Robinson decides
to save, the only course open to him is to make something
over and above what he consumes, either a batch of consumer's goods, which he stores up, or an instrumental
(capital) good. When he acts so, there can be no question
of his supposing himself to be making savings though in
fact none are being made. It may, of course, always
happen that an act of God or the King's enemies destroys
the addition to capital, in which his saving manifests itself,

43

after it has been made. But, subject to this, it is impossible for his decision to save not to realise itself in actual saving, that is in actual investment.

In a pure barter economy consisting of a number of persons dealing together the same thing is true. The representative man, if he decides to save, must either store up something that he has himself made or something which he has obtained from another man in exchange for something that he has made. It is impossible for his desire to save, just as it is with Robinson Crusoe, not to manifest itself in actual saving, *i.e.* actual investment.

In a monetary economy of the kind with which we are familiar an ordinary individual does not, as a general rule, save either by storing up things produced by himself or by expending part of his money income on buying things to be stored up. A business man or a company, out of such part of their income as has not been distributed to shareholders, may, indeed, do this ; and, so far as they do, there is no essential difference between what happens in a monetary economy and in a Robinson Crusoe or a barter economy. In each case whatever anybody decides to save he does in fact save in the form of an accumulation of goods, whether consumption goods or capital goods, and no dis-saving by other people to offset this is set going in consequence of what he has done. Many people, however, save by not spending the whole of their money income and devoting the balance either to increasing their money holdings or to buying through the Stock Exchange already existing securities. We need not trouble about purchases of these or of other already existing pieces of property. For, though particular individuals in our group may buy such things, since to every seller there must correspond a buyer, it is impossible for the group (which we are supposing to be closed) as a whole, and, therefore, for the

representative man of the group to do this.[1] Moreover,
apart from *ad hoc* creations of new money (currency or
bank money), which we need not consider here, exactly
analogous reasoning holds of money balances. Though a
particular individual may increase his money balance, he
can only do so at the expense of somebody else's, which
entails that the representative man of the group cannot
do it at all. Thus at first sight it might seem that in a
money economy, no less than in a Robinson Crusoe or a
barter economy, a decision to save on the part of the representative man cannot work itself out in any other way
than in the actual emergence of real savings.

In fact, however, there is a very important characteristic in which a monetary economy differs from either
of the other two. Though in such an economy the representative man cannot operate his desire to save by increasing his money balance, he can operate it by putting
currency into a stocking or by transferring balances that
have hitherto been active into savings deposits. Suppose
then that he does operate it, or part of it, in that way.
From the point of view of the banks nothing is changed.
Their total deposits and the stock of currency outstanding
from them remains what it was, but the representative
man has in effect drawn money out of circulation, or in
other words reduced the income velocity of money. His
decision to save has not manifested itself in an addition
to the stock of real capital but in a cut in money income.
It has thus failed to accomplish what he intended to
accomplish ; it has been aborted.

This is not the end of the story. If money wage rates
are so plastic or responsive to variations in money income
that employment, and so real income, is not modified at

[1] The representative *Englishman* can, of course, do it so far as he buys
existing securities or other property from foreigners.

all in consequence of the change in money income brought
about by the representative man's action, his decision to
save — the stock of money including bank money in
circulation being given — is *simply* aborted. Real income
is not modified. He has made no real saving. It follows
that his consumption is the same as it would have been if
he had not decided to save; he has cut down his money
income but prices have fallen correspondingly; his real
situation is not altered at all. But if, as is to be expected
in fact, money wage rates and so on are in some degree
sticky, so that, when money income is cut down, employment and real income are cut down also, the representative
man's decision to save is not *simply* aborted. Real
income, as has just been indicated, is reduced and, as a
consequence of this, in all probability real saving is reduced
below what it would otherwise have been. Thus our
representative man's decision to save not only fails to
bring about an increase in real saving. It brings about a
decrease in it and a decrease in consumption at the same
time.

It will be understood that these consequences only
follow so far as the representative man in fact does decide
to save by putting currency into a stocking or by trans-
forming active into savings deposits. If, when some individuals decide to act so, other equivalent individuals
decide in the opposite sense, the representative man does
not decide to do this. Moreover, even if he does so decide,
it is open to the public authorities, through monetary
policy or otherwise, to take countervailing action. For
the present, however, we are not concerned with these
things. It is enough to note that the institution of money
makes possible some *prima facie* important reactions upon
real income and real savings, which could not take place
in a moneyless world.

CHAPTER VIII

MONEY AS AN INSTRUMENT FOR CONTRACTING LOANS

IN any community in the least resembling those we know some stock of man-made equipment, or capital, is an essential element; in most communities we may expect to find additions to this stock being made from year to year by way of investment. A substantial part of the stock of capital has in the modern world been built up by way of loans, and a good deal of the investment by which it is being increased is provided through loans. It is important, however, to be clear in our minds that loans are not *essential* to the building up of capital in the way that investment (*i.e.* saving) is. Indeed, it is quite easy to imagine a capitalist society in which no such things exist; every item of investment being undertaken directly by the person whose resources are invested or by somebody engaged by him at a salary to do this for him. A good deal of investment is, in fact, currently provided in these ways. A business man adds to his equipment or enlarges his factory out of his own income; the directors of a company, acting as the paid agents of their shareholders, 'plough back' a part of the net receipts of their concern in developing its buildings and equipment; a progressive landlord, either personally or through a factor or steward, regularly devotes a part of his income to making capital improvements on his estate. There is no reason in the nature of things why all capital creation should not be undertaken in these ways.

It is true, no doubt, that, if this were done, a number of people who had surplus income and would like to invest might find difficulty in doing so and might, therefore, squander their surplus in forms of consumption that were of little service to them or anyone else. Or they might devote it to forms of capital construction of little productiveness, just because these were accessible to them, to the neglect of other forms that would have yielded a much larger return. These things would plainly entail a social waste. In considerable measure, however, without the use of loans, by means of partnerships, by the establishment of companies financed exclusively from the contributions of ordinary shareholders without any resort to loan capital and in other such ways, what was required could be done. It is, indeed, notorious that in medieval times, when lending at usury was frowned on alike by Church and State, the restrictive effect upon capital formation was greatly mitigated through the use of one or another ingenious device for enabling people to arrange for resources belonging to them to be invested through the agency of others without resort to loans.

Nevertheless, though they are not essential instruments for the accumulation of capital, loans are, for many people, a very convenient instrument for it. A partner exposes his whole fortune to risk, while an ordinary shareholder in a company, though his liability is limited to what he actually subscribes, has no assurance whether he will lose it all, make a small gain, or make a large one. A lender, such as the holder of debentures or of a mortgage, debars himself by the terms of his contract from large gains, but, in return, insures himself more or less effectively against having to put up with *very* small gains or to suffer a total loss. The existence of this kind of opportunity undoubtedly tempts some people into providing capital for investment who would not otherwise do so. Moreover, when the amount of accommodation which particular concerns need varies greatly from time to time, the method of loans is much easier to operate than any other ; so that, once more, the existence of this method is likely to enable more capital to be accumulated than would be accumulated otherwise. Yet again, it enables the allocation of these accumulations among rival uses to be more ' appropriate ', that is, more nearly such that the values of their marginal products will be equal in different uses, than would be practicable otherwise. Partly for these reasons and partly, no doubt, for others, in modern communities a large proportion both of existing capital has been, and of additions to capital is being, provided through the instrumentality of loans. Thus of the nominal capital of British companies, as estimated by Stamp in 1925, 20 per cent was represented by debentures as against 80 per cent by ordinary and preference stock.[1] These figures in the main refer to the financing of fixed capital. As regards working capital, the part played by loans is proportionately much more important. Retailers sell on credit, in effect make loans to customers ; wholesalers do the same by retailers and manufacturers by wholesalers ; while manufacturers themselves and some of these inter-mediaries also in turn rely, for financing their holding of raw materials and half-finished goods, in great measure on advances and discounts from the banks. Thus it may well be that the total money value of loans associated with the financing of working capital — because B relends to C what A has lent to him — is much larger than that of the working capital itself, in the same way that aggregate

---

[1] *The National Capital*, p. 19. In the last estimate published in *The Economist* (January 1940, p. 82) the percentage of debenture capital was slightly higher, but it may well be lower now.

money turnover in a year is much larger than money income. This is important because it means that the failure of one large concern in a line of loans may entail also the failure of many others.

In modern conditions, where governmental agencies, local authorities, special *ad hoc* public boards or the central government itself, often own or operate important industrial concerns, it is not practicable for the required capital to be provided in the way that ordinary shareholders provide part of the capital of joint-stock companies. For, whereas in a broad general way the directors of a company are expected so to conduct their business that the best possible returns are obtained from it, that is do the best they can for their shareholders, a municipal authority, a central institution, such as the post office, or a public board, such as the Port of London Authority, is not expected to act in this way, but, subject to avoiding financial loss, to do its best for the people who purchase the services it renders. Nobody would become an ordinary shareholder in a concern operated on these principles; to do so would be to put oneself at the mercy of the trustees of clients whose interests were directly opposed to one's own. In such cases finance by way of loans embodying definite contracts as to interest and repayment of principal is the only practicable one. It follows that, the larger the part of a country's industry that is run by government authorities as against private enterprise, the more important a part loans may be expected to play in the accumulation and allocation of capital.

So far nothing has been said about a kind of loan that has nothing to do with capital accumulation in the ordinary sense, but has, none the less, in recent years dominated all other kinds; namely, loans raised by central governments for the conduct of war. A large part of these loans is devoted to the construction of war apparatus, factories in which and machinery with which to make this, and so on. Since most of these things, if not destined to be destroyed in the course of the war, are likely to be of little service when peace is restored, such loans are best regarded as consumption loans, not as instruments through which a part of people's income is added to existing accumulations of capital. Resources for war can be, and in the last war in this country were, raised in very large amounts coercively by taxation. But, for reasons into which I shall not enter here,[1] a large part of what is needed is always raised by means of voluntary contributions from the public. It is obviously impracticable for any government to constitute itself into a sort of company and to invite ordinary shareholders to join with it in the enterprise of war, taking as their reward such profit as that enterprise may yield. Whatever evil they may ward off or — most improbably — positive benefit they may bring, modern wars do not, and everybody knows that they do not, yield distributable profits. Apart, therefore, from free gifts, voluntary contributions towards them can only be made by way of loans.

Finally, mention must be made of loans for consumption — other than the loans of goods from retailers to their customers, of which we have already spoken. These, if made by people with a temporary superfluity to people in temporary need, to be repaid when the position of the parties is reversed, may evidently yield substantial social advantages. Such loans are, in effect, though not in name, forms of mutual insurance analogous to insurance against losses by fire, burglary and so on. But, except in so far as insurance companies may make investments, they do not contribute at all to the building up of capital

[1] Cf. *The Political Economy of War*, chap. vii.

In loans to industry or to the government made by the public, what is actually handed over by the lenders is practically always money; and in loans to finance working capital — usually made by bankers — the same thing is true. On the other hand, among manufacturers, wholesalers, retailers and the final buyers of consumption goods what is actually handed over is so much stuff. In all circumstances, however, a valuation of what is handed over is made, the debt contracts being expressed in terms of money. Of such contracts there are a great variety of possible forms : a perpetual annuity of specified annual amount; an annuity of specified annual amount to run unconditionally for an assigned number (which may be *any* number) of years, after which the principal of the loan shall be repaid, maybe at a specified premium, maybe at a specified discount; an annuity guaranteed for a certain period and thereafter redeemable by repayment of the principal, either within so many years or at any time, at the option maybe of the borrower, maybe of the lender ; more complex arrangements under which, as with our national savings certificates, lenders can claim repayment of principal at any time but are granted better terms the longer, up to a specified date, they refrain from doing this ; and so on. When a government borrows to finance a war it always offers a variety of alternative forms of contract so as to bring into its net as many potential lenders as possible. When anybody, private concern or government authority, borrows for capital construction (*i.e.* a municipal gas-works), it usually offers an annuity of specified amount redeemable at its own option not before one and not after another named date. The large extent and the great variety of forms under which resources for investment are provided through the medium of loans contracted in terms of money entails that such consequences as flow from their being made in this form have wide practical, not merely academic, importance.

Of the convenience of loans of this kind, and of their usefulness in helping people, who would like to invest resources over which they have control, in a way satisfactory to them, enough has already been said. We have now to look at the other side of the picture. If no prices ever changed, lenders and borrowers entering into money loan contracts would always get and pay in real terms exactly what they reckoned to get and pay when the contracts were made. But in actual life prices vary. If it were always known beforehand exactly how they were going to vary this would not matter, because the terms of contracts could be adjusted to these foreseen variations. But, of course, future price situations are not known in advance, and, though shrewd guesses are made and play a part in the framing of contracts, the guesses are often astray. This fact was very well illustrated by Irving Fisher in his study of the actual yields in terms of gold of loans of similar types contracted respectively in terms of gold and in terms of silver. Had future movements in the relative value of gold and silver been correctly foreseen, the yield reckoned in either metal must, of course, have been the same with the two types of loan. In fact, during the period studied (1875–95), their yields differed substantially.[1] In like manner, by applying an index of general prices to correct the money yield of a number of loan contracts, Irving Fisher showed [2] that in real terms, owing to incorrect forecasts of future price changes, lenders on several occasions have had to make a payment for the privilege of lending resources, while borrowers have received a *douceur* as a reward for the act of borrow-

[1] Cf. *Appreciation and Interest*, chap. ix.
[2] Cf. *ibid*. p. 67.

ing. Nor are the errors merely random. Prospective
changes in the general level of prices are usually *under-
estimated* both by lenders and by borrowers. Statistical
evidence points strongly in this direction. It is reasonable
to infer, therefore, that downward movements in the
general purchasing power of money, *i.e.* general rises in
price, occurring during the currency of a loan contract
will bring an unlooked-for gain to borrowers who have to
make money payments and an unlooked-for loss to the
lenders to whom those payments are due; and that
contrary movements will have opposite consequences.
Thus large falls in the price level mulct ordinary shareholders for the benefit of debenture holders, and the State,
that is the taxpayers, for the benefit of holders of fixed
interest government loans; and conversely. There is no
reason, I think, to expect that, when large price changes
are taking place, the errors of forecasting will be larger
proportionately than they are with small ones. But, of
course, they, and, with them, the unlooked-for gains and
losses, are likely to be larger absolutely.

These happenings, apart altogether from any consequences to which they may lead, constitute in themselves
a serious defect in the system of loan contracts operated
through money. For they entail interference with people's
plans and with the distribution of income among them, not
directed to any rational end, but purely sporadic. This
has long been recognised, and attempts have been made
to mitigate the resulting evils. Thus on occasions loan
contracts of long duration have been made in terms of
something other than money or in terms of money corrected
by some agreed index number. This idea was incorporated
into the Dawes plan for assessing German reparations
after the first world war, the payments stipulated for in
gold being variable from year to year in accordance with

variations in the general purchasing power of gold. Even, however, if agreement were reached as to the character and content of the index number to be used for measuring general purchasing power, and if the terms of loan contracts were accurately adjusted to this, the ' legitimate expectations ' of borrowers and lenders might still miss fulfilment. For borrowers and lenders might well be interested in different sets of commodities and, if that were so, to make money payments under a loan contract vary with variations in general purchasing power would not entail their varying with the purchasing power of money in respect of either of these two sets of commodities. It might even happen that *both* lenders and borrowers found themselves worse (or better) situated than they had expected to be. Still devices of this kind, as also, of course, successful attempts to keep the general purchasing power of money, as expressed through any reasonably plausible index number, approximately stable, would make money a more adequate instrument for arranging loans than it has hitherto usually been.

CHAPTER IX

THE PURCHASING POWER OF MONEY

WHAT was said at the end of the last chapter about variations in the purchasing power of money calls for a brief supplement. *Prima facie* the phrase 'purchasing power' does not suggest a list of things that some specified pound or other unit of money does buy, but a number of alternative sets of things that it *can* buy. Thus we imagine ourselves confronted with a given fixed set of prices that will remain what they are without regard to the way in which our pound is spent. A pound then *can* buy one apple plus two bananas plus one tin of petrol or alternatively it *can* buy three apples plus one banana plus two tins of petrol. Obviously a very large number of alternative baskets of purchases are open to us. If it were not for the fact that there are certain minimum quantities, different for different things, less than which it is not practicable to buy — melons, for example, may be sold by slices but not apples, radium by milligrams but not tea — the number would be literally infinite. At the back of this concept is the assumption that, while the wielder of our particular pound or small number of pounds is still hesitating, the great bulk of buyers' and sellers' decisions have already been taken. For, if this were not so, we could not be confronted with a given set of prices; whereas, if *all* decisions were already taken, no pound could be confronted with alternatives, but each pound would have to buy what the wielder of it had decided that it *should* buy, that and nothing else. There is clearly a logical awkwardness here. But we need not develop the point. For, though in ordinary speech the term 'purchasing power' may often be used in the way I have been describing, it is not used so in the investigations of economists.

For them the purchasing power of a pound in any period means, not what, with a given pattern of prices, a pound *can* or *could* buy, but what it *does in fact* buy. Since, moreover, different pounds of the community's money income are in fact used to buy different collections of things, *a* pound must mean here, not *any* pound, but some specified pound. We need not, indeed, trouble to distinguish between the different uses in which the different pounds embodied in a single individual's income are expended. But the fact that the representative pound of A's income is expended differently from the representative pound of B's income is very important. There is no such thing as *the* purchasing power of a pound. There is a purchasing power for the representative pound in the money income of any one specified person or group; a particular category of wage-earners, members of the professional classes with money incomes lying between such-and-such limits, people with incomes above £2000 a year, and finally a whole community combined together, as, for example, the citizens of Great Britain. When reference is made to the purchasing power of a pound at any period without further specification, it is the purchasing power of this last pound, that representative of the whole community, which we may normally suppose to be intended. If then, as, with minor qualifications, we have seen to be appropriate, we define money income and real income in such wise that the former is the money value of the latter, the purchasing power of a pound in this sense multiplied by the money income of the community is equal to the real income of the community.

E

The purchasing power of a pound so understood varies from time to time ; and it is of interest to know how much it differs now from what it was at some earlier time. If for any person or group real income were made up of units of one sort of commodity only, or of a variety of sorts the proportionate quantities of which are always the same, there would be no difficulty about this. Real income in 1950 would differ from what it was in 1940 precisely in that proportion. Say then that it changed from Q to mQ. Meanwhile money income of the person or group has changed from I to nI. The purchasing power of a representative pound — what such a pound actually does buy — is thus changed from $\dfrac{Q}{I}$ to $\dfrac{mQ}{nI}$; so that, if we choose to represent it in the first year by 100, in the second it is $100 \cdot \dfrac{m}{n}$. Since, however, in fact real income consists of a great number of different commodities and services, whose quantities are liable to vary in different proportions, variations in the purchasing power of a pound cannot be measured in this simple way. Can these variations be measured at all or, more generally, what is it possible to say about them ?

One thing certainly can be said. If between year 1 and year 2 the quantity of no item comprised in what a representative pound buys has increased by more than x per cent and the quantity of none has increased by less than y per cent, the purchasing power of a pound cannot have increased by more than x per cent or less than y per cent ; if the quantity of no item has increased by less than x per cent and the quantity of none decreased by more than y per cent, it cannot have increased by more than x per cent or decreased by more than y per cent. If the quantity of no item has increased, while the quantity of none has decreased by less than x per cent and the quantity of none by more than y per cent, aggregate real income must have decreased, and cannot have decreased by less than x or by more than y per cent. The limits thus set may turn out in any particular case to be either narrow or wide. If in year 1 the bale of goods representing our pound's purchasing power contained none of a certain item, while that of year 2 contained some of it, the pro-portionate difference between the purchasing powers of a pound in respect of this item in the two years would be infinite. Thus, in that case no limit could be set to the percentage increase in the purchasing power of a pound. Even if there is no item contained in either of our two bales that is not also contained in the other, a change in the quantity of some quite trivial and insignificant com-modity, from say 10 ounces to 100 ounces, would prevent us, even though all the other items were the same in both years, from saying more than that the purchasing power of a pound has not risen by as much as 900 per cent. That is not very illuminating !

Any attempt to go further than this runs at once into an apparently insurmountable obstacle. The purchasing power of a pound, and similarly, of course, real income as a whole, is not a quantity ; it is an inventory. Except, therefore, in the special case where all the items contained in it vary in the same proportion, it is *impossible to measure changes in it in the way that changes in a quantity can be measured.* The quantity of item X included in it has changed between two dates from x_1 to x_2 : that of item Y from y_1 to y_2 ; and so on. This is all that can be said unless we can find some principle in accordance with which it is possible to decide what relative importance shall be attached to proportionate changes in the various items contained in the inventory. So long as we confine

ourselves to the purely physical field, it is clear that no
such principle can be found. There is *no* way of com-
paring the absolute importance in itself of a 10 per cent
change in the quantity of bicycles and of an equal percentage change in the quantity of umbrellas. These
changes have *no* importance in themselves — only in
reference to the states of mind of people. The idea thus
emerges in a vague way that, if we are to measure changes
in the purchasing power of a representative pound in
respect of the inventories of the things that it buys at
different times, we must mean by ' importance ' importance
as a means to the economic satisfaction of the person or
group by whom our pound is spent ; or, more correctly,
as a little reflection shows, importance as a means to such
satisfaction on the assumption that the tastes of the
various members in our group and the distribution of
income among members of different tastes do not change.
To measure relative importance in this sense with any
approach to accuracy it would be necessary to know how
much of their money income people *would have been
willing* to spend on each several item — in one or other
or both of the years between which a comparison is being
attempted. This, however, is obviously impracticable.
We are compelled by lack of knowledge to base ourselves
on how much money they *actually do spend* on the several
items. Weighting by reference to this entails, other things
being equal, giving a smaller weight to changes in items
of inelastic and a larger weight to changes in items of
elastic demand than ' ought ' to be assigned to them if
our object is, as I have suggested it must be, to measure
importance by reference to impact on economic satisfaction, given that tastes are constant. Thus at the very
basis of any structure we may erect there is an incorrigible
flaw. At the best, we shall have to content ourselves with

a makeshift measure, what exactly in the last resort it is measuring being ill-defined and blurred.

Let us then, recognising this, nevertheless adopt, for want of something better, what is actually spent by the group we are studying on the several items that a pound buys as a gauge of the relative importance of the proportionate changes which take place in the quantities of these several items. Immediately we are confronted with a new difficulty. The comparative expenditures of any group, changes in the purchasing power of whose representative pound we are seeking to measure between two years, are very unlikely to be the same in both years. Thus we have to choose between using as weights the expenditures of the first or those of the second year; and clearly there can be no reason for preferring either of these two sets of weights to the other. In view of this it seems reasonable that our index should be constructed in some way that takes account of both sets. But there are a number of alternative devices by which that can be done — for example, the weighted items might be combined either by addition or by multiplication — between which there is no clear ground of choice.

We are thus brought to the threshold of the technical problem of how to construct price index numbers that, for all their inevitable defects in point of logic, shall, nevertheless, be useful in practice. That problem, which I have discussed elsewhere,[1] lies outside the scope of this book. The essential thing to bear in mind is that all purchasing-power indices are necessarily based on *some* assumption about the relative importance of the proportionate changes in quantity undergone by different items. Hence, since no gauge of this, for which absolute rightness can be claimed, is available, they all depend in a measure

---

[1] Cf. *The Economics of Welfare*, 4th edition, Part I, chap. vi.

on convention and arbitrary choice. If we choose, following Irving Fisher, to apply the term ' ideal ' to one among them, we must be careful not to allow ourselves to be misled by it. Strictly, there is no ideal index ; and among a number that can be plausibly defended it is not possible to prove that one is right and another wrong, or even that one is ' better ' than another in any absolute sense. Fortunately — and curiously — experience shows that the results obtained from a number of those most commonly employed are not often widely divergent. Like the members of Lord Melbourne's Cabinet, all of them say much the same thing ; though in this case none of them precisely knows what it is that he is saying !

PART II
MONEY INCOME

CHAPTER I

THE PROBLEM

UP to this point our discussion has been straightforward. We now enter upon more difficult ground. The problem is to disentangle the influences of a general kind upon which the magnitude of money income at any time depends and to show how they interact with one another. It is impossible in a book of this character to attempt a complete discussion of that problem. We have to think away many influences which are at work in real life and to concentrate attention upon a small number that may plausibly be regarded as dominant. Thus I shall ignore the fact that there are a great variety of kinds and qualities of work-people; postulating that they are all alike and all paid the same rate of wages. I shall ignore the fact that there are a great variety of different elements embodied in real income; reasoning as though there were only two kinds, consumption goods and capital goods, all the individual members of each group being physically equivalent. I shall ignore the complications due to labour and capital encountering obstacles and experiencing friction when they try to move from one place or one job to another. I shall ignore the fact that in actual life the size of the population as a whole, and, more particularly, of the population of working age, is continually varying; treating it for the purpose of this analysis as though it were constant. Yet again, until the two last chapters of my book are reached, I shall leave out of account the fact that the several governing factors, to be distinguished immediately, are, on occasions, expected to be different in the future from what they are now. This omission is important, because in actual life this class of expectation is probably in large part responsible for the cumulative upward and downward movements of money income that characterise trade cycles. Finally, in the main part of this enquiry I shall argue as though we had to do with a closed community, reserving what has to be said about international repercussions for Chapter X.

The reader may well feel that a study built on so many unrealistic assumptions cannot have any relevance to the actual world. He is asked, however, to have patience. This model is not created for its own sake. It is a device for enabling us to focus attention, to the exclusion of everything else, upon the interplay of certain deep-seated influences that jointly act upon money income and are, I suggest, *predominant* in determining what it is and how it differs at different times. As has already been emphasised, and is indeed obvious, other influences are at work also. But *these* influences are of outstanding importance. A study of them in a hypothetical situation, where there is nothing to interfere with them, will not, of course, reveal the whole truth, but what it does reveal will be true within limits.

The influences to which I refer are those that lie behind and act respectively through the demand function for real investment; the supply function for real investment; the productivity function of labour, or, more loosely, the coefficient of production; the degree of monopoly exercised in industry, which, for simplicity, I shall regard as independent of the quantity of employment; the function relating the income velocity of money to the rate of interest and, maybe, to other things, to be called the income velocity function; the function relating the stock of money in circulation to the commodity rate of interest, to be called the circulation function; and the money rate of wages. The first four of these sets of influences may be classed as ' real ', the others as monetary factors.[1] In general, they interact together, all of them playing a part in determining alike what happens, on the real side, to real income and the volume of real investment, and, on the money side, to money income and the money rate of wages. This entails, of course, that money here plays a part much more important than that of a mere veil.

The reader will have observed that, apart from the money rate of wages, which is, of course, a quantity, the elements distinguished in the last paragraph are all functions of one or more variables, the functional forms being determined by other influences, some of which, *e.g.* people's general attitude of mind, not being susceptible of numerical measurement, cannot be represented as variables under the function, and some which, though they could be so represented, we find it convenient to deal with otherwise. To some extent it is a matter of choice which of the different relevant influences are represented as variables. How I shall proceed in this matter as regards each of our several functions will appear in due course. The point to be made here is that each of the functional forms is liable to vary

[1] This classification, it may be noted, requires us, if we wish to define ' monetary policy ', to exclude from it such operations by the authorities as dovetailing their demand for public works into periods of slack private demand or budgeting for surpluses in good and deficits in bad times. Monetary policies are policies that operate, to put the matter broadly, not through the demand for, but through the supply of money ; as when the Bank of England buys or sells securities in the market or manipulates the rate of discount, or when the rules governing the maximum permitted issue of fiduciary notes are varied. It should not be forgotten, however, that manipulations of the rate of discount, by affecting people's expectations about the future and their state of mind generally, may also operate to some extent on demand. Mr. Hawtrey lays considerable stress on this.

in all sorts of ways, just as a series of numbers may be varied, not merely by all the numbers changing in the same proportion, but in an indefinitely large number of more complicated ways. To bring into account and investigate the consequences for money income of all these complex kinds of change would be an impossible task. I shall, therefore, confine myself to cases in which what we may call the *level* of one or another function is varied in the same sense over the whole of the range with which we have to do, so that it cannot be more extended in situation B than in situation A over some parts of the range and less extended over others.[1] This limitation of the scope of our analysis is unfortunately unavoidable.

That analysis is also subject to a further important limitation. When any of the governing factors described above is altered, money income does not undergo forthwith a single clear-cut modification. The impact of the disturbance makes itself felt by degrees, setting in motion a *process* that occupies time. To elucidate that process in detail would be too hard a task. What tends to happen after adjustment to disturbances has been completed or, perhaps better, would happen if they were in fact completed, is difficult enough to understand. To do that we have to imagine an initial situation, which either itself represents some sort of equilibrium — in general a short-period equilibrium — or stands in a definite relation to such an equilibrium, and contrast this with the situation which will tend presently to arise out of it if, other things remaining the same, the particular factor whose influence

---

[1] Thus write $\psi(x, y)$ for the function proper to situation A and $\phi(x, y)$ for the corresponding one proper to situation B. The assumption of the text is that, if for any relevant set of values of the variables $\psi > \phi$, this is true of all relevant sets. For some parts of the argument it is necessary to restrict ourselves to the more special case in which for all sets of relevant values of the variables $\psi = m\phi$ where m is a constant. (Cf. *post*, Chap. VI, p. 101.)

we want to investigate is altered in some specified way.
Thus we are not out to determine the full series of consequences for money income which disturbances in our
governing factors actually bring about, but those consequences which they tend to bring about when time has
been allowed for adjustment to be made to them

The most compendious way of investigating problems
of this class is to set out and solve an appropriately constructed set of simultaneous equations. This way was
followed as regards employment in my book, *Employment
and Equilibrium*. Here the analysis, though it has a
mathematical substratum, will be set out in the language
of ordinary life.

CHAPTER II

THE RELEVANT RATE OF INTEREST

In Part I, Chapter VIII, something was said about the way in which, when prices are changing, failures of foresight as to the way in which they are going to change will cause the ' legitimate expectations ' of people who have made long contracts in terms of money to be frustrated. Irving Fisher sometimes [1] uses the term ' real ' to signify the rate of interest in commodities, resulting from contracts expressed in money, that people actually do receive in payment for the service of lending, and contrasts it with what they would have received if, the terms of money contracts remaining the same, prices had remained constant. We are not concerned here with real rates of interest in that sense, except indirectly through the fact that the advantages which high rates confer on business men may react on them psychologically, making them more optimistic about future prospects. The rates that matter directly are rates *ex ante*, not *ex post*. For it is what they expect to happen as a result of present contracts, not what will in fact happen, that affects business men's current demand for, and other people's current supply of, real resources for investment. To avoid confusion, I shall call these *ex ante* rates, not real, but commodity rates.

If the relative values of different things, *e.g.* of apples as against pears, are expected to be the same henceforward as they are now, the rate of interest in respect of

[1] Cf. *The Theory of Interest*, p. 44.

a loan of any assigned length must be the same whether it is expressed in terms of any one or of any other of them. For, were this not so, there would always be a prospect of profit from borrowing in one standard and lending in another. This, of course, holds good if one of our standards consists of money and the other of a representative bale of commodities or, perhaps better, of consumers' goods in general. If relative values are not expected to be the same in the future as they are now, interest rates in different things must clearly differ. Whatever relative values apples — I shall use them to represent our bales — and money are expected to have at different dates in the future, given that the rate of interest in one of them is such-and-such, an equivalent rate in the other can be readily calculated from a generalised formula. For simplicity, however, we may confine ourselves to the very simple case in which it is expected that, immediately after the loan has been made, the money price of apples will change to a given extent, and will thereafter forever stand at the new level.

Consider first perpetual loans in respect of which no repayment of principal will ever have to be made. Let us suppose that the price is expected to change from 1 to p. It follows immediately that the money rate of interest on a perpetual loan must be p times the apple rate of interest.

It is sometimes thought that the relation between interest rates in our two standards for loans of finite length, say n years, is more complicated. On the hypothesis, however, that the price of apples is expected to change from 1 to p immediately after the loan has been made and to remain constant over the period of the loan contract, this is not so. Thus suppose that the period of the loan is n years; that 1 apple, or its equivalent £1, is loaned now; and that under the apple standard it is agreed that one apple, under the money standard that £1, shall be handed to the lender at the end of the n years as repayment of principal. These two repayments will not be equivalent. On the contrary, the repayment under the money contract will be equivalent to $\frac{1}{p}$ times that under the apple contract. Suppose then that each contract stipulated, apart from the return of principal, for a series of equal annual payments over the n years. In order that the two may be equally attractive, the value (whether in terms of apples or of money) of the *annual payments* must be larger with that contract under which the value of what is to be returned as principal is smaller. The difference, however, is wholly due to the fact that compensation has to be made for the discrepant arrangements about what is to be handed over as principal. This compensation is a separate item, having nothing to do with interest. To get at the truth about that we must suppose an apple contract providing for a principal repayment of one apple and a money contract providing for a principal repayment, not of one, but of p pounds. The annual payments contracted for are then rates of interest and nothing else. To make the contracts equivalent, no matter what finite value n has, the rate proper to the money contract must be p times that proper to the apple contract, exactly as it would be if n were infinite, *i.e.* for loans in perpetuity.

What has been said above is the truth, but it is not the whole truth. For, provided that apples can be held from one year to the next at a finite cost, there is a maximum limit which p cannot exceed. Thus suppose that they can be so held at nil cost. Then it is impossible that apples should be lent at a rate of interest less than nothing. Now, if we write r_a for the rate of interest in apples and R_m for the rate of interest plus compensation in respect of principal, stipulated for on a one-year loan in money,

$(1 + r_a)p = (1 + R_m)$.   Hence p cannot be larger than $(1 + R_m)$, or the expected proportionate rise in price, namely $(p - 1)$, than R_m. This, it should be noted, does *not* entail that p cannot be larger than the money rate of interest as I have defined it, namely than the money rate exclusive of any element of compensation in respect of loss of principal.

On the strength of the foregoing analysis we find then that the commodity rate of interest is mechanically related to the money rate of interest in conjunction with current expectations about future price levels. The case discussed above, in which the price level is expected next year and forever afterwards to be higher or lower than it is now by some constant percentage — say 20 per cent — is only a particular instance of a much more general rule. Obviously, if the price level is expected to be 20 per cent up next year and thereafter to go on rising, the commodity rate of interest will fall short of the money rate by more than it will do if prices are expected to undergo no further change. At the other extreme, if the price level is expected to stay forever the same as it is now the commodity rate and the money rate of interest must be identical.

It will be recalled that in the last chapter we ruled out from the main part of our enquiry situations in which the state of any of the governing factors there distinguished is expected to be different in the future from what it is now. It follows that, as regards that part of the enquiry, the price level *cannot* be expected to be different in the future. Hence there is no call to distinguish between the commodity rate of interest and the money rate. They are always equal to one another. This is unrealistic, but it greatly simplifies our task.

There remains the difficulty that rates of interest proper (*i.e.* rates not encumbered by adjustments for

F

incomplete repayment of principal) frequently differ widely for loans of different maturities. It is true that, in this country, cyclical variations being smoothed out, short money rates and long-term rates on fixed interest securities moved very closely together over the sixty years that preceded, and also during the decade that followed, the first world war.[1] But over the period of the trade cycle short-term rates regularly underwent year-to-year fluctuations much wider than long-term rates and sometimes, particularly in the years prior to 1890, not accordant with them in direction.[1] It is thus evident that the rate of interest is a highly ambiguous concept. There is not, I think, any completely satisfactory way of dealing with this difficulty. Keynes' method was to set up a sort of representative rate of interest whose movements may be taken as typical of those of the ' complex of rates '[2] found in real life. Unless the argument is to become impossibly complicated, some such device as this, for all its dangers, is practically forced upon us.

[1] From 1849 to 1909 the average yield of consols was 3 per cent and the average rate of discount on three-months bills was 3·2 per cent. From 1910 to 1921 the two rates were also on the average very near together, though subsequently, and more particularly from 1932, the short rate stood much below the other, the figures from 1932 to 1938 being 3·3 per cent and 0·8 per cent respectively (cf. Morgan, " The Future of Interest Rates ", *Economic Journal*, December 1944, p. 340). As regards year-to-year movements, a chart so drawn that variations in long rates are expressed on a scale several times as large as that used for short rates shows practically no association before 1890, but from that time to the outbreak of the first world war the two series moved similarly and a like association is fairly definite for the decade following 1919.

[2] Cf. *General Theory*, p. 137 *n*.

MONEY INCOME IN RELATION TO THE VELOCITY OF CIRCULATION AND THE STOCK OF MONEY IN CIRCULATION

MONEY income is equal in any period, as it were by definition, to the stock of money in circulation multiplied by what is commonly called the average velocity of its circulation over that period. Its magnitude is thus determined primarily by the sizes of these two elements and ultimately by the influences on which these sizes themselves depend. If the stock of money in circulation is given, the factors that govern the velocity of circulation, if the velocity of circulation is given those that govern the stock of money in circulation, are all that matter. In fact, neither the velocity of circulation nor the stock of money in circulation can properly be regarded as given, so that both sets of factors matter. In the first division of this chapter I shall consider the velocity of circulation, in the second the circulating stock.

I. THE INCOME VELOCITY OF MONEY

There are two senses in which the phrase velocity of circulation has been used, referring respectively to transaction velocity and income velocity. In either case the term velocity suggests movement from place to place of physically distinguishable objects. Units of currency — coins and bank notes — are such objects. It is possible, in principle, by marking adequate samples of shillings, ten-shilling notes and so on, to obtain a statistical estimate of the average velocity with which each kind of currency passes from hand to hand ; and estimates of this kind have in fact been made. But, when money is defined so as to include bank money, which does not, of course, undergo physical movement, velocity of circulation cannot be interpreted or measured in this way. It represents, not — a physical quantity at all, but a ' multiplier '.

The two multipliers, transaction velocity and income velocity, are quite different from one another ; for the reason that a great deal of money turnover is additional to, and lies outside of, money income. Thus consider the making and delivery to me of a pair of boots. The tanner, we may suppose, buys for money his hides from a farmer ; the boot manufacturer buys the resulting leather from the tanner ; the wholesaler the boots from the manufacturer ; the retailer buys them from the wholesaler and at the same time the service of transport for them from the railway company ; and finally I buy the boots from the retailer. The total amount of money entering into all these various transactions is very much greater than the money which I pay for the boots and which represents the sum of the contributions made on account of them to the money incomes of all the persons concerned in these transactions. For the purpose of the present enquiry, therefore, velocity of circulation means income velocity, not transaction velocity.

This velocity, or ' multiplier ', in respect of any year is — this is a tautology — the inverse of the proportion of their money income that people elect to hold on the average of the year as cash and bank balances or, more broadly, as money balances. Since we are here conceiving money income and real income in such a way that money income is the value of real income,[1] this is

---

[1] For an elementary discussion of the relation between money income and real income compare my *Income and Introduction to Economics*, chap. i.

the same thing as saying that the income velocity of money is the inverse of the real balance that people choose to hold in the form of money divided by their real income, or, in other words, the inverse of the proportion of their real income to what they choose to hold in the form of money. To ask, therefore, by what influences the income velocity of money in circulation is determined is the same thing as to ask by what influences the inverse of that proportion is determined.

Now it is plain that, when the rate of interest is given, the amount of real resources that people choose to hold in the form of money must be such that the attractiveness of the marginal apple (apples being taken to represent goods in general) that is held in the form of money is equal to the attractiveness of the marginal apple that is held in the form of real capital. It must be such that the flow of non-material benefit expected from the marginal apple held as money has the same attractiveness as the expected flow of money income in interest from the marginal apple held as real capital. This is so even though no new apples are being invested in one, or maybe in either, of these two uses, so that the marginal apple is marginal to a nil quantity being currently placed in either of them. Nor does it matter that there is no physical conversion of apples into money, but merely a valuation of money in terms of apples ; for, from the point of view of an ordinary individual, when he buys money with an apple, he does, so far as he is concerned, convert the apple into money. Hence the amount of real value, and so, when real income is given, the proportion of real income, that people choose to hold in the form of money, depends partly on how much non-material benefit is yielded by the marginal unit of given quantities of real resources held in the form of money. The greater the non-material benefit that is so yielded, the more

resources people will choose to hold in the form of money
in respect of any given rate of interest — the smaller the
income velocity of money will be.

In this non-material benefit a very important element
is the degree of convenience that the holding of any nth
unit of resources in the form of money yields in obviating
the need for barter, and so in facilitating exchange. How
large this is depends in part upon the time intervals at
which people are accustomed to receive the purchasing
power available for expenditure by them in relation to the
time intervals between their expenditures. Thus, if the
representative man of any group were paid £365 once a
year and expended the same proportion of it every day,
he would get more convenience from the marginal unit
of any given average real balance than he would do if he
were paid the same amount in daily portions of £1 each.

How large this convenience is depends also to an
important extent on how far there are available, for
facilitating exchanges, effective alternatives to money.
Now, a large part of real capital is not owned directly
by individuals in the shape of physical entities, but by
way of various sorts of paper claims. Thus the owner-
ship of a motor works is shared out among ordinary shareholders with a residuary claim on the profits, preference
shareholders and, not to trouble ourselves with legal
niceties, the owners of debenture stock at fixed interest.
More generally, real capital is to a great extent represented
by commercial securities, some of which are readily,
others less readily saleable for money in the market.
There are, besides, claims against the government, which,
though offset by indebtedness from the standpoint of the
community as a whole, nevertheless are capital wealth to
those who own them — War Loan securities, Treasury
Bills and the like. These things are not money as we have

here defined it, but some of them can be turned into money with very little trouble and expense ; they are near-money. Thus in actual life people have not simply the choice between holding resources in the form of money, which yields monetary service and nothing else, and holding them as real capital, which yields an annual material return but no monetary service, *i.e.* is not liquid at all. They have a much more complicated choice among an extensive series of different embodiments of wealth : currency and bank balances on current account, that yield no material return but monetary services only ; bank balances held on deposit account, with a small material return and not quite so liquid ; Treasury Bills, which are very-near-money, with a very small material return ; longer-dated securities, less readily saleable and with a less assured selling price ; and so on down to highly speculative securities or property, such as a house in an out-of-the-way district, which yield practically no monetary service. It is clear that, the more abundant and the more readily obtainable various kinds of near-money are, the smaller will be the convenience yielded to the representative man by the marginal unit of any given quantity of real resources held by him in the form of money.

The amount of convenience yielded by the representative man's holding of the marginal unit of any given quantity of resources in this form depends further on the extent to which dealings between intermediaries are customarily worked through book credits. When a firm buys from one party and sells to another, bills drawn on its debtor may be passed forward to its creditor, so that money is required to discharge only one bill of a given amount instead of two. There are also in vogue many elaborate devices, such as the Stock Exchange Clearing House and the Railway Clearing House, for carrying still further this

method of economising the use of bank money; so that
on the established settling days most debts are cancelled
out and only differences have to be directly met. All this
means that business men have less to gain by locking
resources up in the form of money than they otherwise
would have had. As against it, account must be taken of
the large volume of speculative and other business indirectly associated with industry that is done on the Stock
Exchange and for which, of course, a money basis is
needed.

Besides yielding convenience in affecting exchanges,
resources held in the form of money also serve as a
protective covering to ward off unpleasant consequences
in the event of sudden failures of expected receipts or
sudden emergency calls, and to make provision for un-
expected opportunities for profitable investment, to meet
which by sales of non-monetary property might entail
difficulty or loss. The general setting of industrial
organisation is thus relevant here. It is, indeed, tempting
at first sight to argue that, real income being given, what
goes on inside the industrial machine operates only on the
transaction velocity, not at all on the income velocity of
money; determining how many pounds of turnover a
pound of income shall carry on its back, and nothing
beyond this. But, though, no doubt, the internal organisation of the industrial machine operates to a large extent
on the ratio which the transaction velocity bears to the
income velocity of money, it does not operate solely on
that. If there are ten intermediary dealers, or manufacturers, specialising in successive processes, who stand
between the producers of a raw material and the purchasers of a final product, it is to be expected, in view of
possible bad debts and so on, that a substantially larger
real balance will be needed to bring the non-material

benefit yielded by the marginal unit of it down to what this benefit would be if there were only one intermediary dealer. Plainly, as with convenience, so also with security, the larger the yield of it to be looked for from the marginal unit of any given quantity of resources held in the form of money, the more resources, in respect of any given rate of interest, people will hold in the form of money.

The rate of interest acts on the income velocity of money, in the way indicated on page 77, as a counter-weight to the attractiveness of holding resources in the form of money. Evidently then, other things being equal, the higher the rate of interest is, the smaller the amount of real balances that people hold will be. Hence, *when real income is given*, the larger the income velocity of money will be. This velocity is thus an increasing function of the rate of interest. I should have wished, had it been practicable, to add something as to the probable form, or elasticity, of this function over relevant ranges. For, obviously, the more elastic it is, the greater is the difference to the income velocity of money, and so to money income, that is made by any given difference in the rate of interest. Apart, however, from observing that the elasticity will be greater the more readily available are substitutes for money in the form of one or another kind of near-money, I am not able to say anything about that.[1]

We are thus left with a simple picture of the income velocity of money as an increasing function of the rate of interest, the form, including the ' level ', of this function depending on the extent of the several sorts of non-material benefits derived from real resources held in the form of money. This, however, does not exhaust the

---

[1] The analysis of this section is not inconsistent with current analysis by way of ' liquidity preference '. It is, as it seems to me, a more convenient way of saying the same thing, based on an older tradition.

subject. There is another element, which, while we might, if we chose, reckon it among the influences which govern the form of our function, it is more convenient to treat, along with the rate of interest, as a variable under that function. We saw on page 78 that, the longer the intervals at which a man's available purchasing power is paid over to him, the larger, other things being equal, is the attractiveness to him of holding a large real balance in the form of money; that is to say, the smaller, so far as he is concerned, the income velocity of money is likely to be. Now wage-earners in general receive, not only their money income proper, but also whatever purchasing power may accrue to them by way of transfers under the Unemployment Insurance Acts and so on at substantially shorter time intervals than non-wage-earners. Hence, the larger the proportion of a community's expendable purchasing power that accrues to non-wage-earners, the longer the interval between payments to the representative man will be. It follows that, other things being equal, the larger the proportion of the country's total expendable purchasing power that accrues to non-wage-earners, the smaller the income velocity of money will be. That is to say, the income velocity of money is a decreasing function of this proportion.

There is still a difficulty to be considered. What is the significance of the size of the community's aggregate real income, in itself and independently of such influence as it may exert indirectly through the rate of interest, on the income velocity of money? It seems at first sight that, the larger real income is, the larger this must necessarily be. For the various influences which we distinguished in earlier paragraphs directly determine the *amount* of real resources that people choose to hold in the form of money, and this amount, other things being equal, obviously constitutes a smaller proportion of real income the larger real income is.

Here, however, other things are not equal. As real incomes become larger there is more work for resources held in the form of money to do, just as there is more work for those held in the form of a railway network to do ; so that any nth apple held in this form is more attractive than it used to be. In respect of a given rate of interest, therefore, real balances will be larger with larger than with smaller real incomes ; whence the income velocity of money will not vary in as large a proportion as real income does. It *may*, indeed, be that, when real income multiplies itself n times, the real balance which the representative man chooses to hold will also multiply itself n times. If this were in fact so, it would follow that, when real income varies, no effect is produced directly, *i.e.* otherwise than through the rate of interest, on the income velocity of money. It is, of course, unlikely that a relationship so convenient for analysis is exactly attained in real life. But we may, I think, fairly suppose that something is attained not very different from it ; that, as compared, for instance, with its dependence on the rate of interest, the dependence of the income velocity of money on the size of real income is not appreciably important. In any event we cannot tell whether, other things being equal, it will be made larger or smaller by enlargements in real income. I propose, therefore, to ignore this type of reaction.

2. THE STOCK OF MONEY IN CIRCULATION

I see no reason to believe that *in a closed economy*, such as we have in view here,[1] the size of the community's

---

[1] In an open economy under an international gold standard an enlargement of real income in one country, by causing gold prices there to fall, would tend to attract gold from abroad and, by that route, increase the stock of money in circulation. (Cf. *ante*, Part II, Chap. I, p. 66, and *post*, Chap. X, p. 124.)

aggregate real income has any direct bearing (*i.e.* otherwise than through the rate of interest) on the stock of money in circulation. As with the income velocity of money so here it can safely be left out of account.

The stock of money in circulation, like the income velocity of money, may then conveniently be conceived as a function of two variables, the rate of interest and the proportion of aggregate purchasing power available for expenditure to non-wage-earners.

With a banking and monetary system such as ours, the stock of money in circulation will be larger the higher is the rate of interest ; that is to say, the stock of money in circulation will be an increasing function of that rate. This must not be interpreted to mean that the offer of higher rates of interest tempts the banks into allowing more money to circulate. Rather, the requirements of the community for more money consequent, for example, on the demand schedule for real investment having risen, when they are acceded to, set in motion forces which impel the banks to raise their rate of interest correspondingly. Thus the order of events is, first, a rise (say) in the demand schedule for real investment ; secondly, and consequently, more expenditure in hiring labour accompanied by more employment ; thirdly, a drain from the banks into the circulation, which induces the banks to take action calculated to raise interest rates. This order is illustrated by the fact that in actual life upturns and downturns in employment and money income often precede by a year or more the associated turns in the money rate of interest.[1] Nobody, of course, denies that, if, when the demand schedule for real investment rises, the authorities choose to intervene and alter the function relating the stock of money in circulation to the rate of interest by, for example,

[1] Cf. my *Industrial Fluctuations*, p. 33.

creating new notes, they can secure that the stock of money in circulation is expanded without the rate of interest having to rise at all. Here, however, we are concerned with what will happen if the aforesaid function stays put.

How far the stock of money in circulation will expand in response to given upward movements in the rate of interest — whether the function is a slowly or a rapidly increasing one — depends in large measure on the rules controlling the emission of additional currency. For larger quantities of bank money in circulation in general entail either higher prices or larger purchases, to sustain which more currency is needed in people's pockets. If the rules allow extra currency to be provided fairly readily by new creations, a given rise in the rate of interest will evidently expand the stock of money (bank money and currency together) more than it would do if new creations of currency were either banned altogether or only permitted under severe restrictions. Thus, under an international gold standard, since a rise in the rate of interest would bring gold into the country, and so allow an increased issue of currency, there would be a larger reaction than with a fixed-issue paper currency.

We may pass then to our second variable, the proportion of expendable income held by non-wage-earners. If this is enlarged, the proportion of bank money, as compared with currency, in circulation will also be enlarged ; for the representative non-wage-earner is sure to hold a larger proportion of his money in that form than the representative wage-earner. That entails the withdrawal of currency from circulation into the banking system, where it stands as backing for a total of bank money in circulation several times as large as the withdrawn currency. It follows that the stock of money in circulation is an *increas-*

ing function of the proportion of purchasing power available to non-wage-earners. This is in contrast with the fact noted on page 82, that the income velocity of money is a decreasing function of that variable.

There remains the level, or extension, of the function covering our two variables — whether, in respect of given values of these variables, the stock of money in circulation is larger or smaller — depends ultimately on the policies followed by the State and by the banking system, more especially by the Central Bank; policies which, in this country, have been subject to a long process of historical development. Variations in the level of the function are liable to be brought about under a gold standard by gold discoveries, changes in the gold-reserve policy of foreign governments and so on; under a paper standard by monetary policy and, in the last resort, by government decisions as to the size of the note issue. Variations in these decisions entail, in my use of words, variations in the level of the function.[1]

[1] Thus, if a government decides to regulate the stock of money in such a way as to combat price variations, I say that the level of the function is moved about to that end. It is, of course, equally legitimate to adopt a different convention, as is in fact done in my *Employment and Equilibrium*.

CHAPTER IV

THE DEMAND AND SUPPLY FUNCTIONS FOR REAL INVESTMENT

IF the future return expected from the investment of an nth pound's worth of resources in any year was, say, $\frac{1}{r^{th}}$ part of a £ in every subsequent year, the demand price in interest for an investment of £n would obviously be $\frac{1}{r^{th}}$ part of a £. If the expected future returns are not uniform, but variable, this cannot be so. In that case — and this general case includes also the special case of uniform returns — the demand price is such rate of interest that, if the expected future returns are discounted at it, their present value will be one £. That is to say, the demand price is substantially equivalent to what Keynes called the marginal efficiency of n units of new investment. It follows that the demand schedule for new real investment in terms of the rate of interest is the same thing as the schedule of marginal efficiencies looked for from various quantities of new real investment. The existing stock of capital being given, from our present point of view the quantity of new investment demanded may properly be regarded as dependent only on the rate of interest. That is to say, this schedule represents a function of that one variable.[1] The suggestion that it is also dependent upon the current volume of employment is discussed at length and in the end rejected in my *Employment and Equilibrium*.

[1] Cf. *General Theory*, p. 135.

If in any period the cost of producing the marginal machine, in terms of the quantity of consumption goods that have to be sacrificed for that purpose, is the same irrespective of how many machines are being produced, then, provided that capital is homogeneous, so that the machines produced this year are physically equivalent to those already existing, and provided that the annual output of machines is very small relatively to the existing stock, it will follow that the demand price for new investment in any year must be the same irrespective of the quantity of resources that are being invested ; in other words, the demand curve for real investment will be a horizontal line. This is notoriously out of harmony with common opinion. From a short-run point of view, in respect of periods of boom, the discrepancy is accounted for by the fact that, after a point, the equipment and labour specialised to making equipment will become so fully engaged that further output is bound to encounter increasing cost. There is also the further fact that capital is very far from being homogeneous, so that, when new openings come in sight, the existing stock of the *particular sort* of machines for which they call is in general not large — maybe it is very small — relatively to the annual output of these machines. In these conditions the marginal yield of, say, $2n$ new machines may well be much less than that of n new machines. The general result of these considerations is to confirm the widely held common-sense impression that entrepreneurs will as a rule be prepared to devote more resources to real investment at lower than at higher rates of interest. In other words, the demand curve for real investment in general slopes downward from left to right ; though circumstances are conceivable in which it would be represented by a horizontal, and yet others in which it would be represented by a vertical, line.

The classical economists, it is sometimes asserted, believed the quantity of real income supplied for investment to depend, like the quantity demanded, on the rate of interest alone, and not at all on the scale of real income and so on the volume of employment. This assertion is not, I think, warranted ; and, so far as Marshall, who is commonly reckoned a classical economist, is concerned, it ignores the distinction, which he is careful to draw, between the *desire* and the *power* to save.[1] In any event, it is now generally agreed that the supply of real resources for investment in fact depends, not on the rate of interest only, but also on the scale of real income. Moreover, as I shall argue in a moment, the proportion of aggregate purchasing power available for expenditure to non-wage-earners is also relevant to it. Thus it is conveniently regarded as a function of three variables.

About the relation of the quantity of real resources supplied for investment to the rate of interest there is not complete agreement among economists. Stress has been laid by some writers on the fact that, out of a given real income, persons in certain situations might be willing to supply more real resources for investment in response to a lower than in response to a higher rate of interest. The conditions that must be satisfied in order that this should happen have been studied by Mr. Champernowne in an unpublished mathematical paper. His analysis, based, as it is, on plausible assumptions, may, I think, be taken to confirm Marshall's broad conclusion that, though certain specially situated persons may act in this way, it is very unlikely that the representative man will do so ; he is practically certain to do the opposite. That is to say, the supply of real resources for investment is an *increasing* function of the rate of interest. About the other variables

---

[1] Cf. *Principles*, 5th edition, p. 236.

there is no need to hesitate. Everybody agrees that, other
things being equal, the larger his real income is, the more
resources a representative man will be willing to supply
for investment in response to a given inducement; and
there is considerable statistical evidence to the effect that
the larger a man's real income is, the larger the *proportion*
of it, not merely the larger absolute amount, he will be
willing to supply.[1] It follows immediately that the supply
of real resources for investment is an increasing function
of the volume of real income.[2] This being granted, it is
an easy inference, since non-wage-earners are on the
average substantially better off than wage-earners, that
it is also an increasing function of the proportion of aggregate purchasing power annually available to non-wage-
earners.

About the influences affecting the ' levels ' of the demand
and supply function respectively there is a great deal
that might be said. But the main part of it lies outside
the scope of a book on Money, and a few sentences will,
therefore, be sufficient here. The level at which the
demand function stands depends on business men's
expectations about the returns to be had from different
quantities of investment. These expectations in turn
depend partly upon objective facts ; on whether previously
known openings for investment have been filled or left
free, because, for example, resources, which might have
been invested, have been drawn away to finance a war,

---

[1] Cf. *Employment and Equilibrium*, 1st edition, Part II, chap. vi, § 21.

[2] Real income for this purpose is best measured by potential consumption,
i.e. the flow of consumption goods that would be forthcoming if all work-
people were engaged in making those goods; work-people engaged in off-
setting wear-and-tear of capital equipment being reckoned as indirectly
engaged in making consumption goods. Clearly real income in this sense,
and not actual consumption, which, if the demand for real investment is
expanded, will in some circumstances fall at the same time that potential
consumption grows, is the relevant thing.

on how far inventions and technical advance are creating new openings, and on how far, if at all, government controls over investment are preventing resources from being turned into these openings. They also depend partly on the attitude of the people who direct investment towards objective facts, whether for one reason or another they are looking through rose-coloured or through darkened glasses; whether those of them engaged in different occupations expect that the prices of their product are going to rise relatively to those of other products or to money wages; and so on.[1]   But investment is not undertaken only by private persons.   Government authorities are also large investors, the scale of their demands varying from time to time as public policy is directed, perhaps towards stabilising employment, perhaps towards national defence, perhaps towards some other end.   Total investment demand is thus the sum of public and private demand. It can be affected by deliberate government action; and that in spite of the fact that government demand is sometimes a substitute for, rather than an addition to, private demand, as, for example, when a municipality builds a tramway that would otherwise have been built by a private company.   The level at which the supply function for real investment stands depends primarily on psychological attitudes, which have grown up slowly but are also liable to be influenced by current propaganda in favour of or against thriftiness.

[1] There is nothing to prevent *many* entrepreneurs from entertaining this kind of expectation, while at the same time *no* entrepreneur expects the general level of prices to rise — an expectation the consideration of which we are excluding. (Cf. *ante*, Part II, Chap. II, p. 73.)

CHAPTER V

MONEY INCOME AND DIFFERENCES IN THE
DEMAND FUNCTION FOR REAL INVESTMENT

In this chapter I propose to study the way in which
money income will differ in situation B from what it was
in situation A if all other things are equal but the demand
function for real investment stands higher in consequence,
for example, of a more optimistic attitude on the part of
business men ; *i.e.* is such that, in respect of any given
rate of interest, more resources for investment are demanded
in situation B.

I

This problem is tackled most easily if we suppose, to
begin with, that, in accordance with the view, sometimes
attributed to the classical economists, which was referred
to in the last chapter, the supply of real resources for
investment is a function of the rate of interest only and
not, as in truth it is, of other variables also ; and if, further,
we ignore the fact that the income velocity of money and
the quantity of money in circulation are partly dependent
on other things besides the rate of interest.   On these
suppositions, in the light of what was said in the two preceding chapters about the form of the relevant functions,
the analysis is easy and straightforward.

Obviously, if the demand function stands higher in
situation B than in situation A, the rate of interest must
be higher in situation B.   The extent to which it is higher

will be larger the more elastic is the demand function and the less elastic, in respect of the rate of interest, is the supply function. The rate of interest being higher in situation B, the income velocity of money and the stock of money in circulation must also both be larger in that situation. Each of them will be larger to a greater extent the more elastic is the function related to it. The extent to which either is larger is independent of the form of the other function. That is to say, the consequences of differences in elasticity in the two functions are independent and additive.[1] The ratio of money income in situation B to that in situation A is equal to the ratio of the income velocity of money multiplied by the ratio of the stock of money in circulation. At the same time, of course, the scale of real income and the proportion of expendable purchasing power available to non-wage-earners in situation B are also different from what they are in situation A. But on our present assumptions these differences do not react at all upon the size of money

---

[1] When, as is done on pp. 94-8, reactions through employment and the proportionate share of purchasing power in the hands of non-wage-earners are brought into account, this is, of course, not so. In the face of a given rise in the demand function for real investment it is still true, as in the simpler case, that, the more elastic is either the income velocity function or the circulation function, the more money income tends to rise; but in this case, owing to the reaction through employment and the other variables, the less the rate of interest tends to rise. This entails that the stock of money in circulation increases less — on the assumption that it is an increasing function of the rate of interest — the more elastic is the function connecting the income velocity of money and the rate of interest. By parity of reasoning, the more elastic is the function connecting the stock of money in circulation with the rate of interest, the less the income velocity of money will rise. Thus, the more elastic one function is, the less is the difference made to the effect on money income due to a given change in the demand for real investment by a given enhancement in the elasticity of the other function. If both are made more elastic together the effect is less than the sum of the effects that would have followed from an enhancement in the elasticity of each of them unaccompanied by any change in the elasticity of the other.

income. They are, therefore, irrelevant to, and need not be considered in connection with, it.

2

Let us next, still supposing that the income velocity of money and the stock of money in circulation are functions of the rate of interest only, allow that the supply of real resources for investment is dependent, in the way described in Chapter IV, partly on the scale of real income and partly on the proportion of expendable purchasing power in the hands of non-wage-earners. The conse-quences of a higher as compared with a lower demand function for real investment, that were set out in the last section, will then be modified through the reactions set up in these variables. Such reactions are, therefore, no longer irrelevant to money income, and it becomes necessary to examine them. That is the purpose of the three para-graphs that follow.

The fact that the demand function for real investment stands higher in situation B than in situation A entails, as before, that the rate of interest is higher and, therefore, that money income is higher. This, in general,[1] entails

---

[1] It does not *necessarily* entail this; for two reasons. First, it may be that in industries making investment goods and consumption goods respectively the ratios of the money wages bill to money income are different. If this ratio is smaller in industries making investment goods it may happen that in situation B, where investment is larger relatively to consumption than in situation A, the aggregate money wages bill is not larger — is even smaller — in spite of aggregate of money income being larger. This possibility should be recognised. It need not, however, I think, be taken very seriously. There is no reason to suppose that, looked at by and large, the proportion of income earned by wage-earners as against non-wage-earners from the provision of net new capital is significantly different from the proportion earned by them in serving consumption — which includes, of course, the maintenance intact of the equipment of the consumption goods industries. This is not, indeed, decisive. It is fair to add, however, that, since the amount of labour engaged on behalf of consumption is always much larger

that the money wages bill is higher, and so, the money rate of wages being given, that employment and, consequently, real income is larger.

As regards the proportion of purchasing power available to non-wage-earners the issue is more complex. Apart from transfers, this proportion is the same thing as the proportion of money income accruing to non-wage-earners and may, as a first step, be taken as equivalent to it. Granted then that a higher demand for real investment leads, *via* larger money income, to an enlarged wages bill and so to more employment, does it lead to a larger or a smaller proportion of real, and so of money, income accruing to non-wage-earners? The conditions which must be satisfied in order that it may lead to a larger proportion could be set out mathematically. It is impossible to say *a priori* whether or not these conditions are likely to be satisfied in fact. There are, however, relevant *a posteriori* considerations. Considerable evidence exists to the effect that the proportions of income

than that engaged on behalf of investment, the size of the ratio, money wages bill divided by money income, in the investment industries can only play a small part in determining the ratio, aggregate money wages bill divided by aggregate money income; so that, even if the proportion of resources devoted to investment were twice as large in situation B as in situation A, the ratio, aggregate money wages bill divided by aggregate money income, would still be nearly the same in the two situations. Secondly, even if we had to do with only one set of industries, we could have no absolute assurance that a larger money income must carry with it a larger wages bill. With perfect competition, which, if equilibrium is to be stable, implies diminishing returns per firm, this must, indeed, be so; though it may happen that the ratio, income to wages bill, is smaller with larger than with smaller employment. With imperfect competition, increasing returns per firm are admissible, and *may* act sharply enough to prevent this. But, as will appear immediately, statistical evidence suggests that larger money incomes, the money rate of wages being given, so far from being associated with smaller absolute wages bills, are *unlikely* to be associated even with smaller proportionate ones. These several considerations sufficiently support the generalisation set out in the text.

accruing to wage-earners and non-wage-earners respectively have over long periods, at all events for this country, stood very stable in the face of large disturbances. Thus Dr. Bowley has found that the proportionate share of British income going to property was very nearly the same in 1880 and in 1924, at round about 37 per cent of the whole ; while the proportionate share going to *manual* workers over the whole period 1880–1935 was very nearly the same, from 40 to 43 per cent. Professor Douglas has obtained fairly constant proportions for other countries. Mr. Kalecki has brought together a table according to which the proportionate share of *gross* home-produced annual income going to labour in Great Britain between 1924 and 1935 inclusive was never less than 40·8 per cent and never more than 43 per cent.[1] This high stability in recent history does not, indeed, prove that the productivity function of labour will be, or indeed has been, of such a character that, the degree of monopoly in industry being given, differences in the volume of employment, together with associated shifts in the share of it devoted to investment, *must* leave the proportionate share of income accruing to non-wage-earners unaffected. It may be that what has happened is partly accounted for by shifts that have taken place at the same time by a sort of accident in the degree of monopoly in industry. The historical facts do, however, suggest that moderate differences in these respects are not likely to be responsible for anything beyond *small* changes in the proportionate share of income accruing to non-wage-earners.

This, however, is not the end of the matter. For our concern is not with the proportion of *money income accruing* to non-wage-earners, but, as has been explained, with the proportion of *aggregate purchasing power left*

[1] Cf. my *Employment and Equilibrium*, 1st edition, pp. 148-9.

available to them after account has been taken of transfer payments from them to wage-earners. In present conditions in this country this distinction is made important by the fact that unemployed persons receive substantial payments, drawn in part, indeed, from the incomes of wage-earners still in employment, but in part also from those of the taxpayers, and so of non-wage-earners.[1] This implies that, when employment is good, there is a smaller transfer of real income from non-wage-earners to wage-earners, when it is bad a larger transfer. If then, as we have seen reason to suppose, the proportionate share going to non-wage-earners pre-transfer is pretty much the same with good employment as with bad, their proportionate share post-transfer must obviously be worse with bad employment. We may, I think, conclude with fair confidence that it will in fact be worse then; that, when account is taken of unemployment insurance transfers, smaller employment will be associated with a smaller and larger employment with a larger proportionate share of purchasing power left available to non-wage-earners.

Now we saw in Chapter IV that, other things being equal, the larger is real income, and also the larger is the proportion of aggregate purchasing power available to non-wage-earners, the more resources people will be willing to supply for investment in response to a given rate of interest; and, therefore, the lower the rate of interest and, therewith, money income will be. It follows that, with the demand function for real investment higher in a given measure in situation B than in situation A, money income in situation B is higher to a smaller extent in the conditions contemplated in this section than in those contemplated on pages 91-3. Evidently, however, it cannot

---

[1] For the purpose of our analysis it is convenient to regard employers' contributions to unemployment insurance as a part of the money wage rate.

be smaller to a sufficient extent to make money income actually less in situation B than in situation A.

3

So far we have ignored the fact that the income velocity of money and the stock of money in circulation, besides being dependent on the rate of interest, are also dependent on the proportion of aggregate purchasing power available to non-wage-earners; the former being a decreasing, the latter an increasing function of that proportion. If the relation of the income velocity to the rate of interest is preponderant, the net excess of money income in situation B, as against situation A, will be smaller than we found it to be in the conditions supposed in the preceding section. If the other relation is preponderant, it will be larger. It is not possible to say in general terms which of the two relations is likely in fact to be predominant. But it is reasonable to suppose that their combined effect on money incomes is in general slight.

CHAPTER VI

MONEY INCOME AND DIFFERENCES IN THE
SUPPLY FUNCTION FOR REAL INVESTMENT,
THE PRODUCTIVITY FUNCTION OF LABOUR
AND THE DEGREE OF MONOPOLY IN INDUSTRY

IN this chapter differences in three important influences
from the ' real side ' affecting the scale of money income
will be considered.

1. THE SUPPLY FUNCTION FOR REAL INVESTMENT

It is easy to see that for the level of the supply function
for real investment to stand higher in situation B than in
situation A, that is to say for the quantity of resources
offered for investment to be larger in respect of any given
set of values of our variables,[1] must entail, contrary to what
happens if the demand schedule function stands higher,
that the rate of interest, and so money income, is lower.
The consequences for money income of more thriftiness,
i.e. more readiness to save, are thus opposite in character
to those of an enlarged demand for investment, although
obviously the consequences for the quantity of investment
are similar in character. Thus, other things being equal,
successful economy campaigns leading to greater thrifti-

[1] Some care is needed to avoid confusion here, because, if the quantity
of investment supplied were regarded as a function of the rate of interest
only, and represented by a curve in the conditions set out in the text, the
curve in situation B would lie *below* the corresponding curve in situation A ;
while, nevertheless, with my use of words, the level of the supply function
would stand higher.

ness push money income, and therewith, if money wage rates are maintained, the volume of employment, down, not up. The condition, other things being equal, must not, however, be forgotten here. If an economy campaign promotes business confidence and so enhances the demand for investment, its *total* effect may be favourable to money income. It is only if there is no such reaction on business confidence that it is necessarily unfavourable. There can be little doubt that in the period following the great slump of the early 1930's the campaign was pressed to a stage at which it was in fact unfavourable.

2. THE PRODUCTIVITY FUNCTION OF LABOUR

Three sorts of difference (in the sense of improvements) in the productivity of labour as between situations B and A have to be distinguished. First, technical developments may take place of such a kind that the part of the productive apparatus devoted to making capital goods is enabled to yield a larger output (say 20 per cent larger) of them than before with a given volume of labour and equipment, but the part of the apparatus devoted to making consumption goods is unaltered. Secondly, the part of the productive apparatus devoted to making consumption goods is enabled to yield a larger output than before, but not the part devoted to making capital goods. Thirdly, the parts devoted to making both sorts of goods become more productive in an equal degree. The first and principal stage in our enquiry is to ask how in these three cases the rate of interest will be affected. To make the analysis as simple as possible, I shall suppose that, in view of the smallness of an annual increment of machines compared with the standing stock, the (expected) future return from the marginal machine is the same for all practicable amounts of this increment ;

but that the cost of producing the marginal machine in terms of consumption goods is larger the more machines are being produced. I also assume that the productivity functions, as between situation A and situation B, only differ in such a way that marginal products are different in the same proportions throughout the relevant ranges.[1] This entails that such differences leave the proportion of income accruing to wage-earners and non-wage-earners respectively unaffected.[2]

In these conditions it is easy to see that, in the first of our three cases, when a technical improvement increases the quantity of machines into which a unit of consumption goods converts to m times what it was (m being > 1) in respect of any quantity that may be produced, the quantity of resources demanded for conversion into machines in respect of a rate of interest $\dfrac{r}{m}$ is the same as the quantity that used to be so demanded in respect of a rate r; which implies that more is demanded at a rate r than used to be demanded at that rate. Thus the demand schedule for real investment rises. Hence the rate of interest rises; and hence money income must also rise.

In the second case the whole apparatus, and, therefore, each machine in it, devoted to making consumption goods will, if no further change takes place, henceforward yield an annual flow of consumption goods, say, m times as large as before. But, since a unit of apparatus devoted to making machines only produces the same number of machines as before, the cost of production of any nth machine in terms of consumption goods will also be m times as large as before. It follows that the annual yield resulting from any nth unit of resources invested in machines

---

[1] Cf. *ante*, Part II, Chap. I, p. 68 *n*.
[2] Cf. *post*, Note II, p. 149.

is the same as it was before the change. Therefore, the demand function for real investment is unaffected, and the effect on the rate of interest by way of that function is nil. Real income, however, is increased. This makes people ready to supply more resources for investment in response to any assigned rate of interest. The supply function is more extended. This forces the rate of interest down, and this leads to a reduction in money income.

In the third case distinguished above, the technical improvement is supposed to affect consumption goods and capital goods in an equal degree. The opposed tendencies operating in the two preceding cases are thus both in play, and neither of them is necessarily predominant. The net effect on the rate of interest may, therefore, be either to raise it or to lower it according to the detailed character of the functions involved. Money income will then be larger or smaller according as the rate of interest is raised or lowered.

3. THE DEGREE OF MONOPOLY IN INDUSTRY

When the employer in any firm or occupation is in a position to exercise monopoly power, he cuts down output in such a way that there is a gap between the value of the marginal product that the labour which he employs yields to him and the money wage per unit that he pays to labour. It follows that, in respect of any given quantity of employment in industry as a whole, the exercise of monopoly power carries with it a contraction in the proportionate share of total income (whether expressed in real or moneyed terms) that accrues to wage-earners. We may conveniently measure the degree of monopoly, or imperfect competition, present in the industry of any country by the inverse of the elasticity of demand for the output of the

representative firm of the representative industry.   It can
be shown that, in respect of any given volume of employment, the greater the degree of monopoly in industry the
smaller is the ratio, real wage rate to marginal product of
labour.   Hence, further, the smaller is the proportionate
share of income accruing to wage-earners ; [1] and hence the
larger the proportionate share of income, and probably also
of expendable purchasing power, available to non-wage-
earners.   But, as we saw in Chapter IV, an enlargement
in the proportionate share of expendable purchasing power
so available leads to more resources being offered for
investment in respect of any given rate of interest, therefore to a fall in the rate of interest, and, therefore, to a
fall in money income.   The fall is made smaller than it
otherwise would be by the fact that it itself induces a fall
in the volume of employment, which *pro tanto* makes for
an increase in the rate of interest and so exerts an upward
pressure on money income.   The reactions on money
income consequent on the effects produced by the changed
distribution of expendable purchasing power on the income
velocity of money and on the stock of money in circulation
being partly self-cancelling, their combined effect on
money income is, as was suggested at the end of the last
chapter, probably slight.   Granted that it may be neglected,
the net effect on money income of an enlargement of the
degree of monopoly in industry must be to reduce it.

[1] Cf. *post*, Note III, p. 149.

CHAPTER VII

MONEY INCOME AND DIFFERENCES IN THE IN-
COME VELOCITY OF MONEY, THE STOCK OF
MONEY IN CIRCULATION AND THE MONEY
RATE OF WAGES

IT remains to examine the implications for money income
of shifts, or differences, in what I have called respectively
the income velocity function and the circulation function
of money and in the money rate of wages — all these being
differences, so to say, on the money as distinguished from
the real side.

1. THE INCOME VELOCITY OF MONEY

Suppose that the income velocity function stands higher
in situation B than in situation A, so that, in respect of
any given rate of interest and any given proportion of
aggregate purchasing power in the hands of non-wage-
earners, income velocity is larger in that situation. This
means in the first instance a proportionately higher level
of money income. But, the money rate of wage being
given, that entails a larger volume of employment. This
reacts, as we saw in Chapter IV, to produce a larger supply
of resources for investment and, consequently, a lower rate
of interest. At the same time the reduced level of employment is probably associated with a reduced proportionate
share of purchasing power in the hands of non-wage-
earners. On this account, too, the rate of interest will be
pro tanto lower. Hence the actual income velocity of
money in situation B will be raised above the correspond-

104

ing actual velocity in situation A in a ratio smaller than that in which the income velocity function is raised above it. In other words, when allowance has been made for these secondary reactions, the income velocity of money in situation B will exceed its opposite number in situation A to a less extent than it would have done had there been no such reactions. At the same time, the rate of interest being lower in situation B than in situation A, the stock of money in circulation will also be lower. Hence the proportionate excess of money income in situation B as compared with situation A will be smaller than the proportionate excess in the income velocity of money. There is bound, however, to be some excess.

2. The Circulation Function

Everything that was said above about differences in the income velocity function of money holds good, *mutatis mutandis*, of the circulation function ; and nothing further need be said.

3. The Money Rate of Wages

If it were true, in the manner supposed in the first section of Chapter V, that the supply of resources for investment is independent of real income (and so of the volume of employment) and of the distribution of purchasing power between wage-earners and non-wage-earners, there would be nothing to prevent a rise in the money rate of wages from causing employment to fall as between two situations and at the same time leaving money income unaltered. But that hypothesis, as we have seen, does not agree with the facts. Hence, *if* a higher rate of money wages entails less employment, it must, through the mechanism illustrated in earlier chapters, make the

H

rate of interest higher and, thereby, also make money
income higher.   It has, indeed, been suggested that a
higher rate of money wages need not entail less employment, and that in that case money income will be left
unaltered.   On the assumption that none of the other
governing factors undergoes change, this suggestion is,
as I think, clearly mistaken.   For, if employment is left
unchanged, this implies that both real income and also
the proportionate share of purchasing power available to
non-wage-earners are left unchanged.   In that event,
however, there is nothing to make money income or the
money wages bill change.   Hence, with the money rate
of wages increased, it is impossible for employment to be
unchanged.   Analogous reasoning shows that it cannot
be increased.   Therefore it *must* fall.   But, as we have
already seen, if it falls, money income must increase.
An exactly parallel argument holds good about the consequences of reductions in the money rate of wages.   How
large a proportionate variation in money income a given
proportionate variation in money wage rates will bring
about is determined by the whole set-up of the system.
It will be larger the more a given change in employment,
and so in real income, affects the supply of real resources
offered for investment at a given rate of interest, the less
elastic is the demand schedule over the relevant range for
real resources for investment, and the more elastic are the
functions connecting the income velocity of money and
the stock of money in circulation with the rate of interest.[1]

---

[1] A point of interest bearing on the relation between a money and a real
economy may be added here.   When in either kind of economy wage-
earners try to push wages up, it is presumably real wage rates in which they
are ultimately interested.   Now in a real economy they act directly on those
rates and, if the pressure they exert succeeds, they are bound to force them
up.   In a money economy, however, they cannot aim directly at their goal,
but only indirectly through the money rate of wages.   By forcing this up, as

4

It remains to take note of the special case in which the volume of employment is rigidly fixed either (1) by *force majeure* or (2) by the demand and supply functions for real investment having certain abnormal characteristics.

The case of *force majeure* is simple. If employment is already full — apart from frictional unemployment associated with imperfect mobility — no shift in money income or in the money rate of wages can alter it in an upward direction, while shifts on less than a certain scale can occur without altering it in a downward direction.

The other case may be set out thus. If the demand for real investment is absolutely inelastic, as may happen or almost happen in periods of deep depression, the quantity of employment for investment is by that fact held fixed irrespective of variations in the rate of interest. This does not by itself imply, as is sometimes supposed, that aggregate employment is held fixed. For it is not incompatible with variations in the quantity of employment for the service of consumption; a lower rate of interest combined with a larger real income serving to keep the quantity of resources supplied for investment fixed. If, however, besides the demand for real investment being absolutely inelastic, the supply is also absolutely inelastic in respect of the rate of interest, so that the quantity of resources supplied for investment is the same

we have seen, they make money income rise at the expense, in general, of making employment fall. But this need not in all circumstances entail that their desire to force up real wage rates is accomplished. On the contrary, in conditions of imperfect competition, where increasing returns are compatible with stable equilibrium, the fall in employment *may* be associated with so large a rise in prices that the real rate of wages is lower than it was before. (Cf. an article by Mr. Tsiang, pointing out an error in the first edition of my *Employment and Equilibrium*, in the *Economic Journal*, December 1944, and a reply by me, *ibid.*, December 1945.)

at all rates of interest, this quantity cannot be kept fixed in the face of a change in real income. Therefore, since it *has* to be kept fixed, real income, and so employment, is also fixed. Thus, for employment to be fixed in this manner, there is required, not only an absolutely inelastic demand for real investment, but also an absolutely inelastic supply in respect of the rate of interest. This is a very special combination of conditions, unlikely to be attained completely even in very deep depressions, and need not be considered further.

Suppose then that, employment being fixed by *force majeure*, the proportionate share of real, and so of money, income accruing to non-wage-earners is also fixed. It follows that, with the money rate of wages given, money income cannot be varied. This implies that a shift (difference) in the income velocity function must carry with it such a change in the rate of interest as causes the stock of money in circulation to vary inversely with the income velocity of money; and conversely. A shift in the money rate of wages in like manner must entail such a shift in money income (income velocity multiplied by the stock of money in circulation) that money income divided by the money rate of wages is not varied.

When, however, employment is fixed by *force majeure*, this does not in fact carry with it fixation of the proportionate share of real (or money) income accruing to non-wage-earners. This is not now determined, as it is in normal conditions, by the volume of employment (in conjunction with the form of the productivity function). Adjustment to a contraction in money income or an expansion in money wage rates can, therefore, be made through a fall in the proportion which aggregate income bears to the wages bill, the ratio, wages bill divided by money rate of wages, remaining unaltered

CHAPTER VIII

MONEY INCOME AND COMBINED CHANGES

IN the preceding chapters attention has been concentrated on the consequences for money income of differences in the state of one only of the governing influences distinguished in Chapter I, all the others being assumed to remain fixed. In actual life it may well happen that several of them are varied together. Then the total effect on money income will be equal to the sum of the separate effects of the several disturbances. If, when several types of disturbance are combined, this were always, so to speak, accidental, nothing further would need to be said. But in fact two important types of disturbance, namely variations in the money rate of wages and variations in the stock of money in circulation, are susceptible in some degree of deliberate organised control, so that they can, and sometimes do come about as a reply to other disturbances. Thus, if one of these is tending to make employment bad, the public authorities may try to offset this by bringing about in one way or another an increase in the stock of money in circulation.[1] Again, if one of them is tending to make employment good, wage-earners push harder than usual for higher money wage rates and employers' resistance is relatively weak; and *per contra*, if one of them is tending to make employment bad.

Apart from the limiting case described at the end of

[1] I do not include here action by public authorities designed to stabilise the demand for investment, because such action is directed to prevent a variation in one of the governing factors from occurring, not to cancel the consequences of such a variation by modifying a different governing factor.

the last chapter, expansions in the stock of money in circulation and contractions in the money rate of wages are both in their degree stimulants to enhanced employment and, if introduced alongside of disturbances which threaten to bring about reductions in employment, should make the damage done smaller than it would otherwise have been. This does not, of course, mean that it would be feasible in practice, by manipulating one or other of these elements, to make employment — apart altogether from frictions and imperfect mobility — even approximately stable. It takes time for either sort of manipulation to bring about its appropriate reaction; with the result that, since the foresight of manipulating authorities is always imperfect, corrective action must be somewhat laggard. Moreover, this difficulty carries with it another. Should the pursued stop or slow down, the pursuer is very apt to overshoot his mark. Thus the monetary authority, and the same thing would be true of a general wage authority if one existed, in setting itself to stop a boom, may unwittingly initiate a slump; and conversely. The less carefully the authorities watch the signs of the economic climate and the less swiftly they react to them, the larger will be the extent to which their efforts are frustrated and the less nearly they will succeed in keeping employment stable. Complete success is impossible. This would be so even if it were always practicable to undertake these kinds of manipulation without causing people to expect further manipulations presently; to cut wage rates, for example, without making them anticipate additional future cuts, thus creating expectations which themselves react on employment. In so far as that is not practicable the authorities' task is rendered by so much the more difficult.

This, however, is a digression. For the present purpose what matters is that, when a disturbance in one of our governing factors threatens to make employment larger or smaller, this fact is liable to *evoke* associated disturbances in the circulation function of money and (or) in the money rate of wages, that *pro tanto* offset the threatened change in employment. When, in the face of a fall in employment, the counteracting movement is an upswing in the circulation function of money, money income is made larger than it would otherwise have been ; *per contra*, when money wage rates are cut, it is made smaller.

CHAPTER IX

THE RESPONSIVENESS OF MONEY WAGE RATES

IN this chapter I shall confine attention to the second type of counteracting movements distinguished in the last, that is to movements in the money rate of wages. Suppose that something (other than a shift in the money rate of wages itself) is threatening to lower (or to raise) employment. If the disturbing influence is a movement in the demand or supply function for real investment or in the productivity function of labour, or in the income velocity of money, or in the stock of money in circulation, it acts *through* a decrease or increase in money income. If it is a change in the degree of monopoly in industry, it is *accompanied by* a decrease or increase in money income. These results were established in Chapters VI and VII. Hence for money wage rates to go up in response to bettered, and down in response to worsened, employment entails that they go up in response to increases and down in response to decreases in money income. This implies, in accordance with what was said in Chapter VII, section 3, that, in the face of a disturbance in any of our governing factors, money income is expanded or contracted more than it would be if money wage rates did not respond at all.

To get further than this, we need a new concept, the degree of responsiveness of money wage rates in relation to money income. What precisely in regard to any assigned period of time does this signify? If a governing factor, other than the money rate of wages itself, differs, or, if we prefer it, changes in some specified way between two situations A and B, and the money rate of wages is not altered in consequence, money income will be affected through the processes described in the preceding chapters to a specifiable extent. In these conditions the responsiveness of the money rate of wages may, everybody would agree, properly be called nil. If, on the other hand, the money rate is altered, that rate is responsive in *some* degree. This degree may be measured by the induced percentage change in the money rate of wages divided by the percentage change in money income which would have occurred had the responsiveness of the money rate of wages been nil. We have no right to conclude that the degree of responsiveness so defined will be the same for potential shifts of money income of different sizes. But it is reasonable to suppose that, the more responsive money wage rates are in respect of one size, the more responsive they will also be in respect of other sizes. Hence it is not improper to speak of the money rate of wages being more or less responsive in a general way. We can, however, only specify the degree of responsiveness in regard to potential shifts of a given size. In order, therefore, to carry out a detailed analysis it is necessary to focus attention upon such a shift.

Suppose that, as between two situations A and B, one of the governing factors (other than the rate of money wages) so differs that, with nil responsiveness on the part of money wage rates, money income in situation B would be larger to a given extent than in situation A. If money wage rates are responsive in *any* degree to this change in money income they must rise. This must lead to a contraction in employment, therefore to a decrease in the supply of resources for investment, therefore to a rise in the rate of interest, and, therefore, to a further increment of expansion in money income. Thereupon money wage rates respond by rising a second time and so inducing yet another increment of money income; and so on forever. A rough sketch of what happens can be provided thus. Suppose that, with nil responsiveness on the part of money wage rates, money income would have risen from I to $(1 + a)$I. Make the simplifying assumption that over the range relevant to us every increment kI to money income evokes an increment mkW in the money rate of wages, m thus measuring the responsiveness of the money rate of wages; while every increment hI in the money rate of wages causes money income to expand by an increment phI. It is then easy to see that in the final position the money rate of wages will have increased from its initial

level by $ma\{1 + pm + p^2m^2 + . . .\} = \dfrac{ma}{1 - pm}$W,

and money income by

$$a\{1 + pm + p^2m^2 + . . .\} = \dfrac{a}{1 - pm}\text{I}.$$

In limiting cases this formula obviously agrees with common sense. Thus, no matter what the value of p, if $m = 0$, that is to say if wage responsiveness is nil, money income undergoes the same percentage change, namely aI, ultimately as initially. Again, if $p = 0$, that is to say, if the induced change in the money rate of wages leads to no secondary change in money income, the same thing is true. Finally, if, *per impossibile*, m and p are both equal to unity, so that each upward movement in money income induces an equal percentage upward movement in money wage rates, *and conversely*, money income will go on expanding to infinity! These results are sufficiently plausible to warrant us in drawing out the implications of our formula in more ordinary cases. If the responsiveness of money wage rates is full, while what we may call the inverse responsiveness of money income, namely p, is $\frac{1}{3}$, the ultimate percentage rise in money income will be $\frac{3}{2}a$; with p equal to $\frac{1}{2}$ it will be $2a$; with p equal to $\frac{2}{3}$ it will be $3a$. If the responsiveness of money wage rates, namely m, is $\frac{2}{3}$, the ultimate increases in money income for these three values of p will be $\frac{9}{7}a$, $\frac{1}{2}a$ and $\frac{9}{5}a$ respectively. Always except when $p = 0$ the ultimate rise in money income will be larger the more responsive money wage rates are.

How responsive then are they likely to be in fact? At once we are checked by a difficulty. Even when the variations in a governing factor (other than the rate of money wages) affecting money income are given, the responsiveness of money wage rates is not a single thing measurable by a single figure. It is liable to be different according to the length of time for which the new level of the factor affecting money income has been held, and will probably be more marked the longer the period that we have in view. Thus, when we speak of the responsiveness of money wage rates to changes, or differences, in money income being such-and-such, there is an implicit reference to some specifiable period of time. If we could always specify precisely the period relevant to whatever problem we have in hand, our analysis would be clear-cut. But in fact there are here no hard lines. We cannot even use the distinction sometimes drawn between the so-called short period, in respect of which stocks of equipment are supposed to be fixed, and longer periods; for within the short period so understood there will be sub-periods for which the responsiveness of money wage rates is different. Inevitably, therefore, any picture we can fashion must be somewhat blurred. None the less, a useful distinction to work with is that between the sort of period that is relevant to trade cycle analysis, three or four years, and long-period trends.

Let us begin with the trade cycle period. What can be said about responsiveness from this standpoint? This is

roughly the inverse of ' stickiness ' in money wage rates.
No general discussion of the relevant facts is practicable
in a book of this kind ; for, of course, money wage rates
are responsive in different degrees in different countries at
different times.   I shall, therefore, confine myself to an
account, perforce very brief and sketchy, of the influences
at work in this matter in Great Britain.

As is well known, there is a strong resistance on the
part of wage-earners to downward pressures on money
wage rates.   For a variety of reasons, rather than consent
to money wage rates falling, wage-earners prefer to put
up with a substantially increased measure of unemployment.   Their will and their power in this matter have
both been greatly strengthened by the development of
unemployment insurance and assistance.   Unemployment
does not now drain Trade Union funds in the way that
it used to do, while, at the same time, the situation of
unemployed persons is very much more favourable than
in pre-insurance days.   The forces operating to make
money wage rates sticky against upward movements of
effective demand are less powerful.   None the less,
employers, largely out of fear that wage increases granted
in good times will not be allowed without a stiff fight to
fall again in subsequent bad times, may be expected to
put up considerable resistance to demands for current
increases.   Thus money wage rates are sticky against
upward as well as against downward movements, though
probably in a less degree.

Though sticky, however, there is abundant evidence
that they are far from rigid, *i.e.* totally unresponsive.   Their
general tendency is to follow movements in effective
demand with movements of somewhat smaller amplitude
and after some delay.   On account of the time-lag they
may continue to rise for a few months after money income

has turned down, thus accentuating the turn-down in employment. Thereafter they will follow money income down, the downward movement this time perhaps continuing after money income is turned upwards again, and so helping employment to recover. The fact that during downward movements of the trade cycle employment in general declines and in upward movements expands *progressively* is evidence, for what it is worth, that money wage movements do not merely lag behind, but are also, as has been claimed above, of a smaller amplitude than, the corresponding movements of money income.

It is plain that this stickiness in money wage rates will be *pro tanto* lessened if they are bound by a mechanical link to money income, so that they are forced to move to some extent in accordance with it. Linkages of greater or less stringency have often been arranged over fairly short periods by means of sliding scales connecting money wage rates with prices, in particular with that group of prices represented by the Ministry of Labour's cost-of-living index. In 1922, during the period of rapidly fluctuating prices that followed the first world war, the wages of some three million wage-earners were being regulated by cost-of-living sliding scales. This number had declined by 1939 to one and a half millions. But in 1946, after the second world war, the Ministry of Labour stated that " 2,750,000 wage- and salary-earners are covered by collective agreements which provide for the adjustment of wages in correspondence with movements in the present cost of living index " ; [1] though many of these persons also had their wage rates modified on occasions by means of war bonuses introduced either by agreement or under arbitration.[2] These linkages of money wage

[1] *The Times*, October 25, 1946.
[2] *Labour Gazette*, April 1947, p. 116.

rates with the cost-of-living index *need* not entail linkages
with money income. If the cost of living is deliberately
stabilised by means of various subsidies they *cannot* do
so. But in the absence of this sort of manipulation they
often will.

In any event, however, mechanisms of this character are
little more than *channels* of action. The causal influences
at work are the psychological attitudes of work-people and
employers in conjunction with their comparative strategic
strengths. In this country at the present time there can
be no doubt that over a wide field these influences make
strongly in favour of stickiness — against any high degree
of responsiveness — of money wage rates to variations in
money income from the standpoint of trade cycle periods.
This *pro tanto* restricts the extent to which money income
fluctuates in response to disturbances initiated otherwise
than in the money rate of wages itself ; which implies that
it enhances the extent to which employment fluctuates.

From the standpoint of long-term trends we have to
do with a different kind of situation. This is most clearly
seen if we set before our minds two stationary states alike
in all respects save that in one of them money income
is larger than in the other. It can hardly be supposed
that this superficial monetary difference will cause the
volume of employment in the one to be larger than in
the other. Assuredly wage-earners, having infinite time
at their disposal, will look through the sign to the thing
signified, and will so adjust money wage rates to money
income that the volume of employment is about the same
in both. This does not, of course, imply that in actual
life, with an unchanged population of working age, the
volume of employment on the average, when cyclical
variations are smoothed out, must be approximately
constant. Wage-earners may be thought of as ready to

accept on the average a certain percentage of unemploy-ment as the price of maintaining a certain level of real wage rates. But the chosen proportion will be larger if, for example, unemployed wage-earners are maintained to a substantial extent at the expense of non-wage-earners than if the whole burden of maintaining them falls on other wage-earners.[1]

Apart from changes of this kind we might reasonably expect *a priori* that money wage rates would so adjust themselves as to keep the average percentage of employ-ment over good and bad times together substantially unchanged; as it was in fact substantially unchanged in this country during the sixty years before 1914.[2] This implies that the money rate of wages is, in the long run, fully responsive to variations in the *wages bill*; which, in turn, implies, except as regards shifts in the degree of monopoly in industry, which are liable to induce substantial changes in the ratio between wages bill and aggregate income, that it is not far from fully responsive to variations in money income.

[1] It is thus suggestive that the substantially higher level of unemployment in this country in the inter-war period, as compared with earlier times, was coincident with a greatly expanded system of State-aided insurance against unemployment; though the difficulties experienced in our export industries and the reluctance of employees there to move out of them into others no doubt played an important part.

[2] By reason of this consideration I am myself very sceptical of the widely held opinion that a permanent redistribution of wealth by State grants in favour of the poor would be a remedy for or a palliative of unemployment. Such a redistribution, by diminishing the supply of real resources for in-vestment, might, indeed, be expected to bring about a rise in the rate of interest, therefore to increase money income, and, therefore, unless money wage rates are adjusted, to increase employment. Since money wage rates are sticky, the *immediate* impact of such a policy would almost certainly accomplish that. But, when things had settled down, money wage rates *would* be adjusted; so that, as a long-run anti-unemployment policy, State-enforced redistribution of this kind, however desirable it might be for other reasons, has little to be said for it.

CHAPTER X

MONEY INCOME IN RELATION
TO FOREIGN BUSINESS DEALINGS

So far our analysis has proceeded as though we had to do with an isolated and closed community, no account being taken of international relationships. As everybody knows, in real life these relationships not only exist but play a very important part in the economic life of many countries, and in a special degree in that of Great Britain. When a country is in business contact with an outside world the allocation of labour and other resources inside it are certain to be different from what they would have been otherwise. In general there will be a greater degree of specialisation and a larger real income. Here, however, our concern is not with these things ; rather, with the fact that whatever happens from time to time to money income is, or may be, affected in important ways by these relationships. On the one hand, disturbances, which would have taken place even though the country had been completely isolated, may be made by the fact that it is not isolated to work themselves out differently from what they would otherwise have done. On the other hand, a number of disturbances, which, had we remained in isolation, could not have occurred, may now occur and may affect us in important ways. Under both these heads what happens is likely to be substantially different according as our country's money is or is not tied to the money of the outside world (which for simplicity we may regard as a single unit) by means of a fixed exchange parity, whether established through an international gold standard or in some other way. What follows falls into two parts. The first will study the implications for money income of international business contacts on the assumption that our money is different from foreign monies and that the rate of exchange between it and them is not tied, but free. The second will ask what difference will be made to these implications if our money *is* tied to foreign monies by a fixed exchange parity.

I

Under the former head let us begin with disturbances inside this country of a kind that could occur even if it were completely isolated. Such disturbances may be initiated either on the real side — shifts in the demand function for real investment, in the supply function for this, in the productivity function or in the degree of monopoly in industry —; or on the money side — shifts in the income velocity function of money, the circulation function or the money rate of wages.

Disturbances on the real side, as we saw in an earlier chapter, cause the rate of interest here to rise or fall, and, through that, money income to rise or fall. But the movements in the rate of interest here affect the outside world. If the rate rises, capital is encouraged to flow here, and if it falls, discouraged. As a consequence, the rise or fall in the rate of interest and, consequently, in money income is in a measure damped down.

Disturbances initiated on the money side — our money being independent — cannot set up any international reaction directly. But they can do this indirectly, because, as we have seen, they affect the rate of interest. Thus an expansion in the income velocity function or in the circula-

I

tion function of money causes money income to increase
and the rate of interest to fall. Thereupon foreign capital
is discouraged from coming here ; so that the fall in the
rate of interest is checked and the effect on money income
damped down.   Again a fall in the money rate of wages
leads to increased employment, reduced money income
and a lower rate of interest.   This discouragement against
foreign capital flowing here damps down the fall in the
rate of interest and thereby also at once the fall in money
income and the rise in employment.

Thus in all the cases distinguished so far the existence
of international contacts *damps down*, that is to say,
reduces the scale of, movements in money income here.

Consider next disturbances outside this country of a
kind that could occur even if the country were completely
isolated.   It is evident that disturbances in this group
initiated on the real side must affect the rate of interest
abroad directly ; while those initiated on the money side
— except equi-proportionate shifts in money income and
money wage rates — will do this indirectly by first affecting
real happenings.   But a disturbance in the rate of interest
abroad must affect the tendency of capital to flow to or
away from here ; thus affecting the rate of interest here
and so money income.   Thus in respect of these disturbances the existence of international contacts taken by
themselves always *promotes* variations in money income
here.

There remains a third type of disturbance, *i.e.* disturbances which could not take place at all if this country
and the rest of the world were isolated from one another.
These disturbances consist in shifts in our demand for
foreign goods in terms of our goods and in foreign demand
for our goods in terms of foreign goods.   When a shift
in our demand for foreign goods takes place in consequence

of a shortage or excess in the production of something here, *e.g.* of an abnormally good or bad harvest or of a coal strike, the fact of foreign markets being available to act as a cushion checks the movement of interest rates that would otherwise take place here and so damps down the consequential movement in money income. But shifts in our demand for foreign goods originating otherwise than in this way, *e.g.* through changes in taste, and *all* shifts in foreign demand for our goods must evoke shifts in our real income, so in the rate of interest and so in our money income. That is to say, in these cases the existence of international contacts *promotes* movements of money income here.

In the light of this analysis it is plainly impossible to decide *a priori* whether, for a country with an independent money, the establishment of international contacts tends preponderantly to stabilise or to destabilise money income. The answer in any given situation depends on the detailed circumstances.

2

Turn now to the second part of our enquiry. Given the fact of international business contacts, how will the reactions on money income here brought about in various ways be different if our money, instead of being, as we have so far supposed, independent of foreign monies, is rigidly linked to them, or to the most important of them, at a fixed exchange parity by an international gold standard or some other device of similar effect? The essential fact is that, whereas, with independent monies, the circulation function of money here — the stock of money in circulation in respect of any given rate of interest — cannot be affected at all by international contacts, under a fixed parity system it *must* be affected. It must so adjust itself that prices, at all events the prices of goods that enter into international trade, allowance being made for costs of transport, will be substantially the same here as elsewhere. This implies that the effect on our money income of any disturbances which, with independent monies, would cause the price level to change here, will be *damped down* through an induced international movement of money; while any disturbances which, with independent monies, would cause the price level to change abroad will, through such a movement, *promote* shifts in money income here.

With these broad results as background it may be of interest to consider more in detail three particular cases. First, if an increase takes place here in the money rate of wages, money income, as we saw in Chapter VII, moves in some degree in the same direction, and this *pro tanto* restricts the associated variation in employment. If our money is linked to foreign money this reaction is less marked than it is with an independent money, because, in the former case, but not in the latter, the consequential rise in prices here tends to drive our money abroad. This helps to explain why it was that, until comparatively recently under Keynes' influence, economists paid very little regard to the reactions that reductions in the general level of money wage rates produce on money income or effective demand. So long as the international gold standard was functioning freely, this sort of reaction was probably, in view of the influences we have been describing, quite small. Just as a cut in bricklayers' money wage rates would only affect the *money demand schedule* — to be distinguished sharply from the *quantity demanded* — of bricklayers' services very slightly, so a cut in money wage rates in general confined to one country would only affect very slightly the aggregate money demand schedule for labour in that country.   Hence economists, in neglecting these reactions, were not seriously astray.   With the break-down of the international gold standard, however, the damping-down effect of reactions abroad upon shifts in money income here was greatly weakened.   In these conditions the response of money income to variations in the general level of the country's money wage rates would be much more marked.   To leave it out of account would threaten, no longer a trivial, but, it might well be, a very serious error.   Thus the instincts of the nineteenth-century economists and also at a later date Keynes' conflicting instincts may both have been appropriate to the conditions of their time.   The reader should note in this connection that, whereas, with other types of disturb-ance, if fixed exchange parities are superimposed on international business contacts, money income and employ-ment here are affected in the same sense, with wage dis-turbances they are affected in opposite senses ;   money income being *pro tanto* stabilised, but employment thereby destabilised.

Secondly, should foreigners for any reason become less anxious to buy our exports or, on account, for example, of the onset of an industrial depression, suffer a falling off in productivity in respect of their own export goods, they will not offer such favourable terms for our exports as before.   Nor will the terms be so favourable if British desires for foreign goods are enhanced or British power to buy them, on account of improved productivity, is enhanced.   If our money is not tied to foreign monies disturbances of this kind may be met by shifts in the rate of exchange between, say, sterling and dollars propor-tionate to those that have occurred in the terms of trade. But, if our money *is* tied to foreign monies at a fixed exchange parity, what will happen should the terms of trade for any reason be turned against us to the extent, let us say, of 10 per cent ? This entails that in the new equilibrium our prices, at all events the prices of goods relevant to foreign trade, must be 10 per cent lower than before relatively to foreign prices. This condition would be satisfied without British prices altering at all provided that foreign prices rose 10 per cent. But, in view of the economic predominance of the United States, the presumption is that the main part of the adjusting change would take the form of a downward movement in our prices, brought about by a substantial outflow of money and so a substantial fall in money income here. Of course, if, as has been happening recently, with the rate of exchange fixed, there is a general inflationary situation in the United States, prices here need not fall at all, but, on the contrary, may rise — in an appropriately smaller degree than United States' prices.[1] But this is a separate matter and we do not want to mix up two problems.

Thirdly, suppose that a disturbance initiated on the side of money takes place abroad. If our money is not tied to foreign monies, it will not affect money income here provided that, as will happen if money wage rates and money income abroad alter in equal proportions, it does not give rise to any real disturbance. But, if our money is tied to foreign monies by a fixed parity arrangement, a monetary disturbance abroad *must* affect money income here, even though it does not lead to any real

[1] This combination of circumstances has led to a curious conflict of opinion, some writers suggesting that current circumstances would warrant a *de*-valuation, others that they would warrant a *re*-valuation of sterling in terms of dollars (an increase in the number of dollars against which a pound sterling is sold by our authorities). If what is aimed at is to keep the prices of British-produced goods stable, a rise in American prices less than proportionate to the rise from her point of view in the terms of trade should entail a de-valuation, one more than proportionate to this rise a re-valuation of sterling.

change abroad. Thus, if the price levels of the rest of the world are raised, in consequence, for example, under a gold standard, of the discovery of new gold mines, the output of which is not sterilised,[1] money income here must presently move up in the same proportion as price levels elsewhere. This is not to say that they must move up in the proportion in which price levels elsewhere would have moved up if this country had not existed. Because it exists the outside price movement will have been damped down to some, though, again in view of the predominance of the United States, probably not to a great extent. That, however, is a minor matter. The essential point is that, in whatever proportions prices do change elsewhere, British prices in the conditions supposed must change in a roughly similar proportion, money flowing out or in, in whatever quantity is required to shift money income here enough to bring that about.

The last three paragraphs are a digression from the main theme. Before embarking on it we had distinguished between two sorts of disturbance, those acting primarily on domestic and on foreign prices respectively. We saw

---

[1] During the inter-war period a great deal of the gold that flowed into the United States was sterilised, *i.e.* prevented by policy from forcing up money income in the normal manner. But the most striking application of sterilising technique in recent times had to do with the large money balances — hot money — that were frequently transferred under the influence of political rumour from one country to another. To cope with this there were accumulated in the 1930's, first in this country and afterwards in the United States, large funds of dollars and sterling in Exchange Equalisation Accounts ; these funds being rigidly isolated from the stock of circulating money, so that variations in their volume had no effect on money incomes. They served as vats into which hot money entering the country could be put and from which, when it presently left the country, it could be drawn. There was no difference in principle between this device and the normal commercial device of filling gaps in the balance of indebtedness that were known to be temporary by the use of bank paper. It was in actual fact adopted in this country after we had ' gone off ' gold, but its use is, of course, compatible with the maintenance of an international gold standard.

that, with the former sort, the establishment of a fixed exchange parity tends to stabilise money income here, while with the latter it tends to destabilise it. We cannot say *a priori*, but only with reference to particular detailed conditions, whether disturbances of the one or of the other sort are likely to be larger or more frequent, and whether, therefore, when a system of fixed exchange parities is superimposed upon international business contacts, the effect on our money income will be preponderantly a stabilising or a destabilising one.

3

Since the close of the first world war the impact of the United States, with its enormous economic power, upon world economy has been much stronger than before. The experience of the great slump of the early 1930's, which originated there, fostered the belief that that country's economy is subject to exceptionally violent income and price fluctuations. As a consequence, many people have come to believe that, as things now are, to maintain a rigid exchange parity between sterling and dollars would, on the whole, make for instability rather than for stability in money income here. It is also feared that, if we were to suffer an internally induced depression, the maintenance of rigid exchange parities would seriously handicap any attempt we might wish to make to combat it by means of an expansionist monetary policy, because most of our newly-created money might be sucked away in payment for extra imports or immobilised in foreign-held balances. On the basis of considerations such as these it is widely argued that, whatever may have been the case fifty years ago, in present conditions the maintenance of fixed exchange parities, as under the international gold standard, would be unfavourable to the economic interests of this country.

If, however, in order to insulate itself, Great Britain were to adopt a system of completely free exchanges, it could only do so at substantial cost. The uncertainty and variability of the value of sterling in terms of foreign money would seriously handicap our external trade. For, though it is easy for traders to insure against exchange fluctuations when there is some basic parity about which exchange rates oscillate, where there is no such basic parity that is not at all easy. In any case it is bound to be expensive, and the expense is a barrier against trade. Nor is this all. If one country adopts a free exchange system others may be tempted to do the same; and political pressure, exerted on behalf of the several countries' export industries, may set going a process of competitive exchange depreciation, leading to continuous, rapid and world-wide inflation of incomes and prices; — out of the frying-pan into the fire!

For these reasons it is now generally held that, though a return to the extreme rigidity of the old international gold standard is in present conditions undesirable, nevertheless exchange rates ought not to be left helpless victims of every wind that blows. Once the general long-run balance of international trade has somehow been restored, they should be fixed, within reasonably narrow limits, outside of which no country should be free to pass simply of its own motion; wider changes, if circumstances so alter as to make them *prima facie* desirable, only being permitted with the consent of an international authority established by multilateral treaty. This is the fundamental idea underlying the Bretton Woods agreement.

CHAPTER XI

WAR-TIME INFLATIONS

IT is characteristic of war-time — the history of the two
world wars in many countries provides abundant proof —
that money income is always expanded and, also in some
degree, inflated in the sense defined in Part I, Chapter III.
In the earlier stages of a war, when the slack normal to
peace-time is being taken up, unemployment disappearing
and people who would normally be at leisure coming into
income-yielding activity, a substantial proportion of the
expansion is likely to be balanced by increased work on
the part of productive agents. The inflation will be a
good deal less than the expansion. But, when once war
gets fully into its stride, there is little scope for taking up
further slack. Whatever further expansion in money
income takes place after this stage has been reached will
be inflationary expansion : in a long enough war expansion
and inflation become substantially the same thing.

Up to a point the process of such inflations is very
similar to what happens in a strong industrial boom,
associated with the development, say, of railways or of
electrical appliances, and fortified by gathering optimism
on the part of business leaders. There, too, we find expansion of money income and inflation of it taking place
together, the inflation being less than the expansion in the
earlier stages and nearly or quite equal to it in the later.
None the less, there is a very important difference on the
monetary side between peace-time booms and war. Peace-
time booms are, in general, subject to a restraining force,

which, if nothing else meanwhile interferes, must ultimately bring them to an end.   As money incomes rise,
and, therewith, either prices or the quantities of things
bought, people need more and more currency in their
pockets for the conduct of ordinary business.   But in
modern banking systems there are always blocks or brakes,
which limit the volume of currency that may be issued ;
and in peace-time governments and Central Banks have
in the past been extremely chary about tampering with
these.   Hence after a time, to protect the reserves of
currency and ensure that these shall not fall short of
what is required to enable all valid cheques to be cashed
when presented, the banking system must force up rates
of discount and sell securities in the market, persisting in
these practices till the boom is brought to an end.   In
war-time nothing like this can happen.   The government
needs money from the banks and if, as an indirect consequence, people require more currency, it is bound, on
pain of its war effort breaking down, to authorise the
creation of more currency.   This dam, so formidable in
peace-time, is in war-time completely swept away.   So
long as war lasts there is no chance whatever that the
inflation will be brought to a halt, or even to a pause,
by impact on it.

Among inflations or inflationary expansions of money
income in their war-time manifestations there may be
distinguished three forms, or rather three aspects, which
may be generated and developed separately, or may, two
or all three of them, be combined together.   I shall call
them respectively deficit-induced inflation, wage-induced
inflation and galloping inflation.   I am not wedded to
any of these names ; but the distinguishing characteristics
which they are supposed to represent are important, and
to have *some* names for them is useful.

Consider first deficit-induced inflation. In war-time the government is bound to undertake very large expenditure for war purposes. It endeavours to raise funds to meet this expenditure by taxes and loans (not themselves financed by new money) from the public. It may happen, however, that the public, being unwilling to reduce its consumption and private investment sufficiently far, does not provide it with enough funds to enable it to purchase a sufficient share of the available real resources. To fill the gap the government possesses itself of new money created for it by the banks, with the help of which it is able to obtain control of whatever share it chooses. So long as government expenditure exceeds the yield of taxes and loans (not themselves financed with new money) from the public, more and more new money has to be created and the upward movement of money income must continue.

An almost inevitable concomitant of this is a rise in the money rate of wages. Up to a point that rise is a pure defence mechanism, through which wage-earners, when aggregate money income is moved up, secure that their own money income shall rise in the same proportion as other people's, thus preventing real income from being transferred from them for the benefit of non-wage-earners. This sort of rise is not either itself a cause of new money being created or a secondary stimulus making the amount created larger than it would otherwise have been. Thus, if aggregate money income is raised by 10 per cent through the creation of new money, the fact that, employment being constant, wage-earners' incomes are raised by 10 per cent along with the rest, instead of other people's being raised by more than 10 per cent, has no tendency to evoke yet more new money or to cause aggregate money income to rise again.

Turn next to wage-induced inflation. Wage-earners in war-time may ask for increases of pay to offset rising prices when these are due to diminished *productivity*. This, it must be clearly understood, is quite a different thing from the diminished *production* of civilian goods which results from resources being diverted away from them to war uses. So long as no new money is created, that does not make the prices of civilian goods rise, because, to match the decrease in these goods, there is a corresponding decrease in money income available to spend on them. Diminished *productivity* is diminished yield of goods for a given quantity of resources engaged in producing them. It is bound to come about in war-time on account of the forces of destruction and obstruction which are then let loose. This is particularly true in a country like England, where a great deal of what people consume is produced, not directly, but indirectly by means of exports exchanged for foreign goods brought here in ships. If 10 per cent of our imports are sunk on the way, this means, in effect, that the efficiency of productive resources engaged in making the exports with which to buy them is reduced by 10 per cent. Thus, even if there is no increase in money income, prices are likely to rise ; so that wage-earners are strongly tempted to ask for higher money wage rates. If wage rates for all industries were negotiated in common, the knowledge that increases in them would entail increases in general prices might act as a powerful deterrent. But in fact wage rates are negotiated separately in different industries ; and the effect of a wage increase in any one of them taken by itself on *general* prices would be small. Hence the prospect of it will not influence negotiations much. One or two industries then are likely to ask for and secure rises. Thereupon workers elsewhere seek parallel rises, so as to maintain their old relative position. This stirs up those who secured wage increases first to new efforts, and a snowball effect is generated. Indeed, even apart from this, in view of the strong strategic position in which war places them, they might well ask for them. Now it was shown in Chapter VII that in normal conditions, with the income velocity function and the circulation function of money given, money wage rates (for work of given quality) could not be forced up without employment being reduced. But in war-time it is proper to assume that increased wage rates will not be allowed to evoke unemployment. Hence wage rises are a cause of new money being created and so of a rise in money income and prices. If then money wage rates are raised again to offset income and price rises, the same effect is repeated ; and so on for-ever.

It is important to realise that this type of inflation may arise and develop even though the government is financing the whole of its expenditure out of taxes and loans from the public (not themselves financed by new money) — what a recent Chancellor of the Exchequer conveniently, despite the fact that all savings, if savings at all, must be genuine, called " genuine savings ". It cannot, therefore, be prevented by the government refusing to finance itself by creations of new money. Granted that full employ-ment is to be maintained, the forcing up of money wages in the way described above must lead to higher costs, and so to larger incomes backed by new money, which, if it is not created for the government, must be created for private persons. The only way in which this type of inflation can be prevented is by stopping the upward race of wages against prices.

What, then, is a government confronted with this situation to do ? Some critics claim that the problem is simple; increases in money wage rates have merely to be forbidden by law. Provided that no new money is being created for other reasons, this will, no doubt, accomplish its purpose. But it is not politically practicable to allow at all events the poorest class of wage-earners to suffer even those cuts in real income that are the ' natural ' consequence of a war-induced decrease in productive efficiency. The State can only hope to prevent increases in money wage rates if it either makes grants to specially poor persons (*e.g.* through children's allowances), or, by means of subsidies, prevents the prices of things needed by them, in regard to which productive efficiency has diminished, from being raised in correspondence with their money costs. Either of these policies entails State expenditure. If this expenditure can be financed out of genuine savings — so called — the inflationary movement is successfully stopped. Suppose, however, that it has to be financed out of new creations of money. Then wage-induced inflation is stopped and deficit-induced inflation substituted for it. There are two advantages in this. First, the rate at which new money has to be created under the deficit-induced inflation, which is the same at the outset as the amount that had to be created under the supplanted wage-induced inflation, will remain constant, whereas with the wage-induced inflation it would grow continually larger, because wage increases entail price increases, which in turn lead to further wage increases. Secondly, deficit-induced inflation can be arrested by filling up the deficit, whereas wage-induced inflation, unless the chasing of wages after prices is prevented, cannot be arrested by any means whatever.

There remains galloping inflation. As we have seen, money income depends, not only on the total stock of money in circulation, but also on the frequency with which a representative unit of it appears as income, that is to say, upon its income velocity. In ordinary circumstances this velocity is stable within reasonably narrow limits. But in war-time, as also in the difficult periods that immediately follow wars, this stability may completely break down. If money incomes move at more than a certain speed and prices do the same, people become distrustful of money. There thus comes into play a type of influence which in the formal analysis of earlier chapters was ruled out of account.[1] People expect that more and more money is going to be created — that the circulation function of money is going to rise and go on rising. Hence there takes place a flight out of money into goods, that is to say a great increase in income velocity, and so a rise in money incomes much more rapid than the associated rise in the stock of money. There is a fever, which, so to speak, feeds on itself; every rise in prices entailed by rising income carries with it more distrust, a more rapid flight from money and a further rise in incomes and prices; this in turn making necessary more and more rapid creations of new money to finance the enlarged costs of government purchases. This cumulative movement is still inflation. But it is an especially virulent type of it deserving a special name. After what degree of severity a primary inflation, whether wage-induced or deficit-induced, will turn into galloping inflation depends on the temperament and past experience of the people concerned. It is probable that a much higher degree of severity would be needed in this country than in one of the many that were recently victims of a currency break-down. But even here a primary inflation, no matter though it were associated with a fairly substantial increase in activity and output, that involved a doubling of money income in two or

[1] Cf. *ante*, Part II, Chap. I, p. 66.

a quadrupling in four years of war, might be dangerous. On the other hand, with one entailing a 50 per cent rise in money income in two years and a 100 per cent rise in four there would be little risk of the inflation beginning to gallop. Obviously an inflation that does gallop is an extremely serious thing. As the experience of Germany and other countries in the 1920's abundantly showed, it may well be the harbinger of chaos. If it were to set in during the actual course of a war it might entail dis-organisation so great as to make military victory impossible. Thus, when the need to fill government deficits or the upward pressure of rising wage rates generates an inflation, the crucial question is whether that inflation is or is not large and rapid enough to give rise to a flight from money, and so to evoke galloping inflation.

Let us suppose for simplicity that wage-induced inflation has been effectively controlled, whether by being trans-formed into deficit-induced inflation or otherwise, or, at all events, that it has been reduced within narrow limits ; so that deficit-induced inflation is the only type of primary inflation with which we have to deal. On this basis, con-sider a situation in which the income velocity of money is roughly constant at about 2, *i.e.* in which the money income of six months is about equal to the stock of money in circulation — more or less, the normal pre-war situation in England — ; and then suppose that over a period of four years the money income of each six months has to be supplemented, to meet the exigencies of war, by creations of new money bearing equal proportions to the then existing stock of money in circulation. In what degree, in the absence of any flight from money, will money income have expanded ? The answer to this question, for any given proportion of new money creations per six months, can be expressed in the simple formula set out

K

below.[1] This yields the following inferences. If the government takes command, by issues of new money, over one-half of the productive resources of the country in each six-monthly period, money income must double every six months; standing after two years of war at 16 times, after four years at 256 times its original amount! If the share of the country's resources, of which the government takes command every six months by this means, is one-quarter, money income will be multiplied by 3·2 at the end of two years, by 9·9 at the end of four. With the share at one-sixth the corresponding multipliers are 2·1 and 4·3 ; at one-tenth 1·5 and 2·3 ; at one-twentieth 1·2 and 1·5. Clearly then more than one-twentieth of the country's real income could be absorbed by the government annually for war purposes *via* new money without appreciable risk of galloping inflation ; as much as one-quarter could not be.

The practical inference is plain. A government engaged in total war and anxious to secure itself against galloping inflation must continually press to obtain the bulk of the money that it needs from the public by taxes or loans — taxes or loans not themselves furnished by the public out of new creations of money. To this end it may obstruct, through systems of rationing, priorities, licences, prohibition of new private capital undertakings and so on, alternative uses for private funds. By issuing

---

[1] If $\frac{1}{n}$ be the fraction of the country's real income continuously absorbed by the government through the creation of new money, and r be the number of six-monthly periods during which this has happened, money income will stand, on the assumptions here adopted, at $\left(\frac{n}{n-1}\right)^{r}$ times its original amount. In this method of attack certain assumptions are involved which are very unlikely to be realised in practice. But the substitution of alternative more complex and perhaps more plausible assumptions makes much less difference than might at first sight be supposed.

various types of war loan adjusted to the tastes of different classes of people it may encourage subscription to them. It may either openly, or in the form of taxes on which reimbursement is promised after the war, raise forced levies. It may — though there is much to be said against this — offer high rates of interest. It may appeal to patriotism and adopt all manner of propagandist devices. About the detail of what it can most usefully do there may well be differences of opinion. But the broad lines are plain. Resort to all other means of keeping itself in funds should be pressed ; resort to creations of new money under no matter what guise, whether by the government itself or by the people from whom it collects funds, should never be allowed to play more than a small part in providing for its needs.[1]

[1] Some parts of this chapter are taken from my article on " Types of War Inflation " in the *Economic Journal*, December 1941.

CHAPTER XII

A CHEAP-MONEY POLICY

UNDER this title I do not include the policy of making
money cheap in periods of depression and dear in periods
of boom, so that the average level of money rates over
good and bad times together is not much affected. The
purpose of that policy is to make money income and,
through that, employment more stable than it would
otherwise have been. I mean the policy of holding the
representative money rate of interest (or, better, the complex of rates), on the average and on the whole substantially
below the level at which it would have stood in the absence
of intervention ; the policy, in brief, which Mr. Dalton,
as Chancellor of the Exchequer, explicitly undertook to
pursue. Such a policy has obvious attractions for State
Treasuries, since it at once enables the existing floating
debt to be financed cheaply, keeps low the cost of new
government borrowings and enables the annual charge
in respect of old borrowings at high interest, when the
date at which they become repayable arrives, to be reduced.

In the last paragraph I was careful to speak of the
representative money rate of interest. It is important to
realise that, when a government engages in a cheap-
money policy in our sense, and, to carry that through,
forces down short money rates (*e.g.* by offering Treasury
Bills very cheap), it cannot in general depress the *representative* money rate nearly as much as it does short money
rates. This is well illustrated by the fact, that, whereas
in this country over a long period prior to 1929, when

there was no question of a cheap-money policy, the yield of consols and the market rate of discount on three-months bills were on the average of good and bad times very nearly the same, from 1931 onwards, when the cheap-money policy first won favour with the Bank of England, short money rates were never above 1 per cent and long rates never appreciably below 3 per cent.[1] Holding short money rates at a very low level is an *instrument* of cheap-money policy, but the degree to which the complex of rates as a whole moves is for our purpose the significant thing.

It is always in the power of the State to keep the representative money rate of interest down by making it illegal for people to invest in some undertakings in which they would have liked to invest. In an all-out war such restrictions are sure to be imposed so as to prevent urgently needed real resources from being withdrawn from the war effort to uses which, from a national standpoint, are less essential. In the aftermath of war, when many forms of reconstruction work are called for, there is much to be said for continuing these restrictions. State action of this kind cuts down the demand for investment, or, more accurately, cuts down the part of that demand which is allowed to manifest itself in action. The root purpose of such policies is to prevent scarce resources from being dissipated, so that they may be conserved for essential needs. A necessary consequence is that money interest rates do not rise so high as they would otherwise have done. But this is an *incidental* consequence. The *object* of the restrictions is to make investable resources available where they are chiefly needed, not to keep money interest down. Though, therefore, they serve as important props to a cheap-money policy when they are used alongside of it, they are not a

[1] Cf. *ante*, Part II, Chap. II, p. 74 *n.*

part of that policy, as I understand it here. That policy could be operated, or, at all events, attempts could be made to operate it, quite independently of them. To bring out its essential character I shall assume in what follows that it is in fact being operated without any accompanying restrictions upon permitted investment, or rather — since, if investment abroad were completely free, the policy would almost certainly break down — upon permitted investment at home.

Let us, to make things clear, imagine that public policy is directed to hold the representative money rate of interest below the level at which it would normally stand, say at 2 per cent in conditions such that, apart from this intervention, it would have stood at 4 per cent. The monetary authority, we suppose, announces that henceforth its agents, *e.g.* the Bank of England, will always lend money, created, if necessary, for the purpose, not merely for short- but for long-term loans, at that rate of interest ; and that it is proposed to go on expanding the stock of money to any extent that that policy may require. It is beyond doubt that, by this procedure, the monetary authority, if it wishes and if its profession of intentions is believed, has power to hold the money rate of interest down to 2 per cent. For, when anybody, able to offer suitable security, can borrow at this rate from the central source, he will not be so foolish as to pay a higher rate elsewhere. Supposing then that the policy succeeds in its purpose, we have to investigate its implications.

It may perhaps be thought at first sight that, while the money rate of interest is made different from and lower than it would normally have been, the rate expressed in terms of any chosen bale of commodities — the commodity rate, to speak broadly — will be unaffected ; so that, if, for example, both these rates had previously been 4 per cent, the money rate will be brought down to 2 per cent, while the commodity rate will be the same as it would have been if the money rate had not been doctored. In Chapter II, as the reader may remember, it was observed that for the main part of our enquiry, differences between money and commodity rates of interest would not need to be taken into account because we should not be considering disturbances that entail expected future shifts in any of our functions and so expected changes in prices. For the purposes of this chapter that limitation does not hold. For the adoption of a cheap-money policy is likely, on the face of things, to create an expectation that the circulation function will presently be modified; so that the commodity rate and the money rate of interest are not tied together. Hence the suggestion made at the beginning of this paragraph cannot be rejected out of hand, but must be considered on its merits. Now, we saw in Chapter II that the commodity rate cannot be greater than the money rate unless it is expected that prices in the future will be less than they are now. But, should the government adopt a cheap-money policy, this is much more likely to create an expectation of rising than of falling prices, because of the likelihood that it will lead to an increase in the stock of money in circulation. Hence, instead of the commodity rate of interest not being cut down as much as the money rate, it is likely, if anything, to be cut down more.

It is plain then that an enforced reduction in the money rate of interest will cause more real resources to be demanded for investment. To meet this extra demand, if no effect is produced on aggregate employment, either because employment is already ' full ' in a literal sense or for any other reason, the extra resources for investment will necessarily be raised at the expense of consumption.

There will be ' forced levies ' from consumers for the service of investors. In so far as employment is increased relatively to what it would have been otherwise, consumption will not be depleted by forced levies, but the extra resources required for investment will be raised out of extra real income at the expense, if we like to put it so, of increased employment or, more paradoxically, of diminished leisure. The presumption is that in actual life some of the required resources will come from reduced consumption and some from augmented real income. In any event the rate at which real investment takes place over the average of good and bad times together will be larger than it would otherwise have been.

To carry the enquiry a little further let us assume that the cheap-money policy is firmly maintained, that nothing else intervenes and that complications due to investment being made in part from motives other than the expectation of interest,[1] may be ignored. We may conveniently distinguish three cases. For the first, when the cheap-money policy is introduced, the economic system is standing in a classical stationary state, the commodity rate of interest being equal to the representative man's rate of time preference. In such conditions the new rate at which loans can be raised being, *ex hypothesi*, lower than that, some net real investment will take place ; whereas, had monetary policy not interfered, there would have been no net investment or disinvestment. Moreover, investment will continue to be undertaken year after year until the commodity rate of interest, the money rate and the rate of time preference, which there is reason to expect will fall as real income grows,[2] all coincide. At this stage

---

[1] For these complications cf. *Employment and Equilibrium*, 1st edition, Part II, chap. vi.
[2] *Ibid.*

then a new stationary state establishes itself and is thereafter maintained, with a larger real income — because the stock of equipment is larger than the original one — and with all three rates standing at 2 per cent.

Let us suppose, secondly, that, when the cheap-money policy is introduced, the economic system has not reached a stationary state, but the commodity (and money) rate of interest exceeds the rate of time preference, so that some net investment is being undertaken every year. In these conditions the economic system is in process of movement towards a future stationary state with a definable stock of capital and rate of interest. The rate of interest initially ruling being 4 per cent, let 3 per cent be the rate that would rule if the ' natural ' goal were attained. It is easy to see that the introduction of a cheap-money policy decreeing a permanent money rate of 2 per cent will speed up the date at which the stock of capital attains the level which it would finally attain apart from this policy. If at that stage the policy were abandoned, no further investment would be made, but the stationary state with a 3 per cent rate of interest would establish itself. If, on the other hand, the 2 per cent policy is still maintained, what follows will be exactly on the lines indicated in the preceding paragraph. In the end a stationary state with a 2 per cent rate of interest and a stock of capital appropriate to that will, or, rather, apart from the dislocations which in practice will inevitably take place, *would* be attained. The final goal reached is, as in the last case, different from what it would have been in the absence of the cheap-money policy.

Thirdly, let the situation be as described in the last paragraph, save that the stationary state towards which the economic system was tending when the cheap-money policy was introduced was one embodying a rate of interest less than 2 per cent, say 1 per cent. It is then plain that the enforced introduction of a 2 per cent money rate will speed up the expansion of the stock of capital and the scale of real income, until they reach the levels at which the rate of interest would have become 2 per cent in the normal course of events. After that the further forward movement to the final 1 per cent stationary state takes place exactly as it would have done had there been no interference. The goal is reached earlier but it is not different from what it would otherwise have been.

All this, however, is aside from our main interest, which has to do with money income. We must now return to that. While the public authorities are engaged in holding the money rate of interest below what it would normally be, otherwise than by forcibly cutting down the demand for investment, they are bound continually to create or to secure the creation of, new money, in order to fill the gap between the resources for investment demanded and those supplied, which at the enforced low rate of interest would otherwise manifest itself. Provided that consumption is rationed and prices controlled, a good deal of the new money may presently be moved into savings deposits, so that the income velocity of money is reduced and money income does not expand much. Apart from controls, however, it *must* expand and must, moreover, continue to do so so long as the money rate of interest which the public authorities have decided to maintain stands below the rate which would have established itself apart from their intervention. In view of the serious social disadvantages which the large and rapid rise in general prices consequential upon that would entail, the public authorities will be exceedingly anxious to prevent such a rise. Hence the strenuous pursuit of a cheap-money policy will tempt them to maintain these restrictions much longer than would otherwise be necessary ; maybe even permanently. Since, however, it is not feasible in practice for controls to be applied to all parts of the economic field, it may well happen that where they are *not* operating the pressure of money demand forces up prices to fantastic heights. This indirectly impels an undue proportion of our productive resources to seek those favoured fields, thus creating shortages elsewhere. The damage brought about in these ways when attempts are made to escape from a continuing inflation of money income by the erection of controls may be very serious. Scylla and Charybdis have each their menace. If a strenuous cheap-money policy is maintained, to escape from both is impossible.

NOTES

I

Some light on the subject-matter of Part I, Chapter V can be thrown by the use of a simple diagram. We suppose that the rationed article is being produced in a perfect market operating under conditions of competition. Draw SS′ to represent the supply schedule, the surrounding conditions and the period of time involved being such that this curve cannot be inclined negatively. Draw DD_1 to represent the demand curve of the market in the absence of rationing and DHD_2 to represent it when maximum rations are fixed. It is then obvious that in respect of prices so high that nothing is consumed the two curves coincide.

As prices fall the successive points on DD_2, which always lies inside DD_1, lie further and further away from it because the ration limit becomes effective for more and more people. When the price

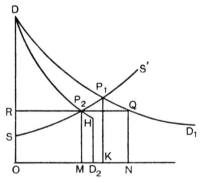

falls so low that everybody purchases the whole of his permitted ration the curve becomes a vertical line, say HD_2, indicating that no more can be purchased however low the price falls. Let DD_1 intersect SS′ in P_1 and DD_2 in P_2; and through P_2 draw a horizontal line RP_2Q cutting DO in R and DD_1 in Q. Then, if rationing is imposed but no maximum price is fixed, actual consumption

is measured by OM, the maximum consumption allowed under the rationing scheme being OD_2 and the consumption that would have taken place had there been no rationing being OK. Given the price

148

P_2M, MD_2 measures the quantity of permitted ration that the market has not wanted to buy at that price; and MN the amount which at that price it would have wished, but is not allowed, to buy. Obviously the lower SS' lies — since it cannot be inclined negatively — the larger are OM, OK and ON.

If on top of a rationing system, under which the demand curve is represented by DHD_2, a maximum price is fixed equal to P_2M, no effect at all is produced. If one greater than P_2M is fixed the actual price will be below it, so that again, on the assumption of a perfect market, no effect is produced. But if one less than P_2M is fixed (unless P_2M and the maximum price are both less than HD_2) equilibrium will be ruptured, so that the quantity of commodity offered for sale is less than the quantity that people wish and are permitted by the rationing scheme to buy. If the maximum price is also a minimum price and if it is fixed at more than P_2M some of the commodity available for sale will be left unsold on the producer's hands.

II

NOTE TO PART II, CHAPTER VI, PAGE 101

The statement at the end of the first paragraph on page 101 can be proved as follows. Write x for the stock of labour at work, and, the stock of capital at work being taken as fixed, $m\,F(x)$ for output, when m is a constant. Write η (defined as positive) for the elasticity of demand for the output of the representative firm of the representative industry. (For the significance of this, see *Employment and Equilibrium*, 1st edition, Part II, chapter i, § 6.) Then the proportion of aggregate output (income) accruing to wage-earners may be written

$$\frac{m\left(1 - \frac{1}{\eta}\right) x F'(x)}{m\,F(x)}.$$

This is obviously the same for all values of m.

III

NOTE TO PART II, CHAPTER VI, PAGE 103

With the same notation as in Note II write also w for the money rate of wages, and p for money price. Then for equilibrium

$$w = p \left(1 - \frac{1}{\eta} \right) . F'(x).$$

$$\therefore \frac{w}{p} = \left(1 - \frac{1}{\eta} \right) . F'(x).$$

But $\frac{w}{p}$ is the real rate of wages and $F'(x)$ is the marginal product of x units of labour. Therefore, for any value of x,

$$\left(1 - \frac{1}{\eta} \right) = \frac{\text{Real wage rate}}{\text{Marginal product of labour}},$$

and, as indicated in the preceding Note,

$$\frac{\left(1 - \frac{1}{\eta} \right) x F'(x)}{F(x)} = \text{the proportionate share of output accruing to wage-earners.}$$

Both of these expressions are obviously smaller the larger is $\frac{1}{\eta}$.

THE END